First printed 2008
Eaglemoss Publications Group, 1st Floor, Beaumont House, Kensington Village,
Avonmore Road, London W14 8TS

While every care has been taken in compiling the information in this book, the publishers cannot accept responsibility for any errors, inadvertent or not, that may be found or may occur at some time in the future owing to changes in legislation or for any other reason.

The expression of Best as used in the title of the book is the trademark of The National Magazine Company and The Hearst Corporation, registered in the United Kington and USA, and other principal countries of the world, and is the absolute property of The National Magazine Company and The Hearst Corporation. The use of this trademark other than with the express permission of The National Magazine Company or The Hearst Corporation is strictly prohibited.

The Best website is www.bestmagazine.co.uk.

ISSN 1759-0205
123456789
Reproduction by F E Burmans, UK.
Printed in the EU by Imprimerie Pollina.

BEST Food Fast!
Tasty Chicken
Front cover: EM/Steve Lee; 3 EM/Steve Lee, 8 Simon Smith/Best/NMC, 9 Ian Garlick/Best/NMC, 10 EM/Karl Adamson, 12-13 Alamy/Brand X, 13(c) EM/Karl Adamson, 13(b) Ian Garlick/Best/NMC, 14 EM/Steve Lee, 15 EM/Karl Adamson, 16 Simon Smith/Best/NMC, 17 EM/Karl Adamson, 18 Ian Garlick/Best/NMC, 19 Getty/Dorling Kindersley, 20 EM/Howard Shooter, 21 EM/Steve Lee, 24 Thomas Odulate/Best/NMC, 25 EM/Steve Lee, 26-27 Ian Garlick/Best/NMC, 28-30 EM/Steve Lee, 31-32 Ian Garlick/Best/NMC, 33-36 EM/Steve Lee, 37-38 Ian Garlick/Best/NMC, 39 EM/Steve Lee, 42-47 Ian Garlick/Best/NMC, 48-49 EM/Steve Lee, 50 Simon Smith/Best/NMC, 51 Ian Garlick/Best/NMC, 52 EM/Steve Lee, 53 Sian Irvine/Best/NMC, 55 Simon Smith/Best/NMC, 56 Ian Garlick/Best/NMC, 57 EM/Steve Lee, 58 Sam Stowell/Best/NMC, 59 Sian Irvine/Best/NMC, 62 Ian Garlick/Best/NMC, 63 EM/Steve Lee, 64 Mary Rose Loyd/Best/NMC, 70 EM/Steve Lee, 71-73 EM/Steve Lee, 74 Ian Garlick/Best/NMC, 75 EM/Steve Lee, 78 Ian Garlick/Best/NMC, 79 Sian Irvine/Best/NMC, 80-81 EM/Steve Lee, 82-83 Ian Garlick/Best/NMC, 84 Anthony Blake/Best/NMC, 85 EM/Steve Lee, 87 Sian Irvine/Best/NMC, 88 Simon Smith/Best/NMC, 89 EM/Steve Lee, 90 Ian Garlick/Best/NMC, 91 EM/Steve Lee, 94 Sian Irvine/Best/NMC, 95-97 Ian Garlick/Best/NMC, 98 EM/Steve Lee, 99 Mary Rose Loyd/NMC, 100-101 Ian Garlick/Best/NMC, 103 Mary Rose Loyd/Best/NMC, 105-109 Ian Garlick/Best/NMC; 110 Simon Smith/Best/NMC, 111 Mary Rose Loyd/Best/NMC, 113-120 Ian Garlick/Best/NMC, 123 Thomas Odulate/Best/NMC, 124 Ian Garlick/Best/NMC, 125 EM/Steve Lee, Ian Garlick/Best/NMC

EM = Eaglemoss Publications Group
NMC = The National Magazine Company

Visit www.best-cookery.com
or call us to subscribe or buy missing books
UK: 0871 277 0097
South Africa: (011) 265 4307

best food *fast!*

Tasty Chicken

best food fast!

If your family is anything like mine, we'd be lost at meal times without our humble chicken. We'll often have a delicious roast with all the trimmings for Sunday lunch – then use the leftovers to rustle up salads, curries, pasta or a stir-fry during the week. Even the carcass makes a stock for soups and sauces. In fact there isn't once ounce of the bird that we don't use – a great way to cook tasty meals that don't cost the earth.

So I'm delighted that the first cookbook in this series is all about Tasty Chicken.

Inside, you'll find over 75 tasty recipes to tempt the family. We've kept them as quick and easy as possible, using only a handful of everyday ingredients available from your local supermarket.

There are also 100s of tips and easy-to-follow guides for basic preparation techniques – from cleaning to jointing to carving. So your cooking experience is as simple and waste-free as possible.

I really hope you enjoy the book and it becomes as invaluable in your home as it has become in mine.

Let's get cooking…

Michelle Hather
Editor

best *food fast!*

CONTENTS

Chicken Makes a Perfect Meal

Our favourite poultry, chicken has lean and tender meat that makes it perfect for a huge range of recipes, as well as being low-fat and healthy.

Chicken used to be a real luxury – a once-a-year treat – but now it's an everyday food that often finds its way to our dinner table. This is good news, as chicken is packed with nutrients. It is an excellent source of:

- protein;
- minerals (such as calcium, copper, iron, phosphorus, potassium and zinc);
- vitamin A and the B vitamins.

Chicken is an all-round favourite for a family tea-time or dinner party.

A LOW-FAT FOOD

As well as essential nutrients, chicken also contains less saturated fat than red meat, especially if you remove the skin, where most of poultry fat can be found. The white meat of a chicken breast is the leanest cut and to reduce fat further, you can choose a cooking method that adds little or no extra fat, such as:

- poaching;
- stir-frying;
- grilling;
- roasting.

A VERSATILE INGREDIENT

Chicken can be used in a variety of ways. It's ideal for a traditional Sunday roast, yet it can also be cut up and prepared with a huge array of sauces from around the world. So whether you're in the mood for a hint of the Orient with a Sweet-and-Sour Chicken or prefer a European classic such as Italian Chicken with Olives and Peppers, there is always a way to prepare it that will tickle your taste buds.

EVERYONE'S FAVOURITE

Perhaps the biggest benefit of chicken is that it's an all-round favourite, whether for a family tea-time, or a dinner party. It's easy to cook, too. So, whatever the occasion, you're sure to find the perfect chicken recipe here in *Tasty Chicken*.

HOW MUCH IS ENOUGH?

Whether it's a meal for one or a large gathering, there's a chicken that will do the job. If you're planning to cook a big bird, make sure that it'll fit in your oven! You should plan to provide 350g (12oz) of chicken meat per serving. Here's a guide to how much a whole chicken will provide:

POUSSIN	1 SERVING
DOUBLE POUSSIN	2 SERVINGS
900G–1.3KG (2–3LB) CHICKEN	2 SERVINGS
1.3–2.25KG (3–5LB) CHICKEN	4 SERVINGS
2.25–3.5KG (5–8LB) CHICKEN	6 SERVINGS

■ EXPERT TIP

When using meat from a chicken breast, be careful not to over-cook it as lean meat can quickly become very dry.

Know Your Chicken

Nowadays there is such an array of chicken on offer, fresh or frozen, it can be confusing to know which to choose. Here's a guide to what's on offer.

The flavour and texture of a chicken will depend on how it was raised and fed, and on how old it was when it was slaughtered (see Chicken Types, opposite). For example, a free-range chicken will have a more intense flavour than a battery chicken. The younger a chicken is when slaughtered, the more tender it will be. The older the chicken is at slaughter, the more flavour it will have. Use meat from younger birds in recipes that call for frying, grilling or roasting, while meat from older birds is best for braising or stewing.

CHICKEN JOINTS

While chickens are sold whole they are also sold already jointed into separate portions. These are, of course, more convenient for the busy lifestyles many of us lead today. You can buy them as:
- halves or quarters;
- breasts;
- thighs;
- drumsticks;
- wings.

Chicken is also sometimes sold as fillets, which is chicken meat removed from the bone. A chicken breast that has been deboned and skinned can be flattened into an 'escalope'.

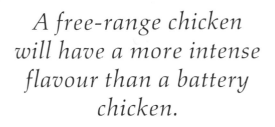

EXPERT TIP
If the giblets are sold with the chicken, you can put them to good use to make a delicious stock or gravy.

A free-range chicken will have a more intense flavour than a battery chicken.

Chicken Types

This breakdown covers the terms used to describe a chicken, depending on how old it is or how it was raised.

WHAT'S ON OFFER	WHAT IT'S LIKE
OVEN-READY CHICKEN	An oven-ready chicken has had the feathers plucked and the giblets (the innards) removed. Most chickens are sold oven-ready.
FREE-RANGE CHICKEN	A free-range chicken has been allowed to wander and forage for food. It is treated more humanely than a battery-farmed bird and will have a more varied diet that will affect its flavour.
BATTERY CHICKEN	A battery chicken is confined to a limited amount of space and can only eat the food it is given, which is usually fishmeal; although it will not be as full of flavour as a free-range chicken, it's a cheaper alternative.
CORN-FED CHICKEN	A corn-fed chicken has been fed a special diet, which generally gives the bird a yellowish colour. This kind of chicken has a plump and juicy meat.
SINGLE POUSSIN	A single poussin is a 4–6 week-old chicken that weighs up to 250g (9oz) and serves one person. Because it has little flavour, it is often stuffed and served with a sauce. Sometimes it is flattened in a method known as spatchcocking.
DOUBLE POUSSIN	A double poussin is a 6–10 week-old bird that weighs up to 350g (12oz); it serves two and has a little more flavour than a single poussin.
SPRING CHICKEN	A spring chicken is a 10–12 week-old chicken that weighs about 450g (1lb). It also serves two and has a similar amount of flavour as a double poussin. It is a good choice for roasting.
ROASTER	A roaster is more than 3 months old and weighs 900g–1.8kg (2–4lb). As a whole chicken, it's a good choice for roasting and braising, and it can be jointed to use in a recipe where chicken is grilled, baked, fried or stewed.

The Basics for Handling Chicken

When you buy your chicken, there are several things you should know about handling and storing it.

Like all poultry, chicken can contain certain bacteria – such as salmonella and campylobacter – which are often linked to food poisoning. However, if you store, handle and cook chicken properly, the chicken will be safe for eating.

PICK A HEALTHY BIRD

The first step is to choose a healthy chicken. You should look for:
■ moist skin that hasn't been broken and without any dark patches;
■ plump-looking breasts;
■ a fresh smell – if the bird smells 'off' don't use it.

Always check the 'sell-by' date if you buy your chicken from a supermarket.

STORING CHICKEN

Once you buy chicken, try to get it home and into the fridge or freezer as soon as possible – consider using a cool-bag to carry the chicken home in hot weather. You'll probably be tempted to put a fresh chicken straight into the fridge. However,

Check the 'sell-by' date if you buy your chicken from a supermarket.

the best way to store your chicken is to first remove its plastic wrapping and wipe it all over, inside and out, with kitchen paper – remove the giblets first. Place the bird on a plate and cover it loosely with some clingfilm or greaseproof paper.

By taking such steps you will help prevent bacterial growth. Now the chicken is ready to be stored at the bottom of the refrigerator for up to two days. By wrapping it in clingfilm you will stop the meat drying out or picking up the flavours of other food nearby.

FROZEN CHICKENS

Before buying a frozen chicken, make sure that it is frozen solid. It will keep in the freezer for up to three months. Always defrost a frozen chicken completely before use, preferably in the bottom of the fridge.
■ Place the chicken on a plate to catch any drippings.
■ For a bird that weighs up to 2.25kg (5lb), plan on 24 hours for defrosting.
■ For a larger bird, allow about 30 hours.
■ When thawed, there should be no ice crystals inside the chicken's body cavity and you should be able to wiggle the legs. Cook the bird as soon as possible.

What to Remember...

When handling raw chicken – or any other type of poultry – you need to follow certain hygiene rules:

■ Don't let raw chicken come into contact with cooked food in the fridge.

■ Always store chicken – along with any other raw meat – on the bottom shelf in the fridge to avoid drippings contaminating other food.

■ Always wash your hands in hot soapy water before and after touching the meat.

■ Thoroughly wash any surfaces or utensils used for trimming raw chicken, including knives and work surfaces, before preparing other food with or on them.

■ Keep a separate chopping board exclusively for preparing raw meat. It's a good idea to label the board.

■ Make sure the chicken is cooked thoroughly to kill all bacteria. To check it's done, pierce the thickest part with a skewer – the juices should run clean, without a trace of red.

■ Never store a chicken prepared with stuffing – this can allow bacteria to develop in the stuffing that won't be killed off by the lower temperatures necessary for cooking a stuffed chicken.

Cutting up a Chicken

You'll need to follow only a few simple steps to be able to joint a whole chicken successfully.

Chickens bought from a supermarket already cut up into portions make life easy for the busy cook but, weight for weight, they are much more expensive than buying a whole bird. By jointing a chicken at home, you save money and also get the trimmings for making your own stock (see page 21).

DIVIDE AND CONQUER

There are a number of ways to joint a bird; it's really up to you and the number of people you are feeding. By following the two sequences shown opposite, a chicken will yield eight fairly even-sized portions.

■ Cut the wings with some of the breast attached to make them meatier.

■ Either leave the legs whole or divide each one into thigh and drumstick.

■ If you want to remove the skin, simply pull it away from the meat end to end.

   Remember that for casseroles, it is best to leave the leg portions on the bone (and sometimes the breasts as well) to keep them in shape.

SECRETS TO SUCCESS

■ Use a sturdy kitchen knife with a medium-length blade that's sharp enough to slice through the flesh and joints.

■ Use a heavy board that won't slide about.

■ Feel for the ball and socket joints with your fingers so you can cut cleanly between the bones.

JOINTING A COOKED CHICKEN

Sometimes it's easier and quicker to serve cooked chicken with a sauce rather than make a casserole. As with uncooked chicken, it's cheaper to joint a whole bird than buy it in portions. The procedure is the same – except that the cooked pieces come away more easily. Remove the drumsticks first, then pull away the thighs. Slice the breasts from the breastbone, then pop out the wing joints.

■ EXPERT TIP

There are two nuggets of meat, called oysters, on the underside of the bird. Turn the chicken over and find them midway down the backbone.

JOINTING THE LEGS The first four portions come from the chicken's legs. You can cut the portions with the skin on, and you can leave the legs on the bone.

1 Position the chicken with the breast side up. Holding one leg, cut the skin between the body and thigh. Push the leg out, popping the thigh bone from its socket, then cut through the joint to remove the whole leg. Repeat with the other leg.

2 To separate the thigh from the drumstick, position one leg with the inner thigh up. Cut down firmly between the thigh and drumstick and through the knee joint to produce two pieces. Repeat to divide the other leg.

3 Cut through the joint between the drumstick and scaly knuckle end. You now have four good-sized chicken portions.

REMOVING BREAST & WINGS The other four portions come from the chicken wings and breast. A part of the breast is cut with each wing to make the portions even in size. After jointing, there will still be enough meat left on the carcass to make a good stock.

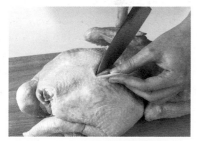

1 To joint the wings, start by slicing diagonally across the wide end of each breast. Make this cut on both sides of the bird before releasing the wings from the carcass.

2 To separate each wing, with its attached piece of breast, feel for where the wing is attached to the carcass and cut firmly through the joint. Trim off the pointed tips of the wings at the nearest joint.

3 To cut the breast pieces from the carcass, feel for the breastbone between the two breasts and slice down on one side of it. Working with small strokes of the knife, keep it against the ribs to cut free a breast portion. Repeat for the other side.

Roasting a Chicken

Poultry is often cooked in the oven, and one of the most popular
ways to cook chicken is by roasting.

Whole chickens are ideal for roasting in the oven. You can truss the bird to help maintain a compact, neat shape as it cooks, but it isn't essential. Adding a stuffing will help the breast meat stay juicy and succulent, and will add flavour to the chicken.

CHOICE OF STUFFINGS

The breadcrumbs in a stuffing provide the perfect neutral background for a range of sweet, savoury and spicy flavourings. Stuffings may incorporate sausagemeat or bacon, onion, garlic and at least a couple of freshly chopped herbs. (For additional ideas for flavouring a roast chicken, see page 20.)

COOKING TIME

**When calculating how long to roast a
chicken, remember to include the weight
of any stuffing. If you place the chicken
breast side down for the first 30 minutes
or roasting time, this will help keep the
breasts moist by encouraging the juices
to run into them.**

TEMPERATURE	200°C/400°F/GAS 6
TIME	15–20 MINS PER LB
BASTE	EVERY 20 MINS

EXPERT TIP

Turn a roasted chicken carcass into stock. Just put it into a large pan and cover with water. Bring to the boil, then simmer for about an hour.

STUFFING A CHICKEN

A stuffing can be made the day before cooking and refrigerated, but it must be at room temperature when stuffing the bird. It is traditional to cook the stuffing inside the chicken, but never pack it too tightly or the bird may not cook properly.

■ First wipe the inside of the bird clean with a kitchen towel.

■ Pack a small amount of stuffing in the neck end, fold over the flap of skin and hold it secure with a skewer.

■ Place more stuffing in the body cavity and close the cavity by tying the legs together with string.

■ You can cook any extra stuffing in an oiled baking dish – you'll then have a meat-free stuffing suitable for vegetarians.

CARVING TIME

Let the chicken relax on a hot dish for 10–15 minutes before carving. Start with the legs when you carve the chicken, cutting through the skin between the leg and breast. Pressing the thigh down will help expose the hip joint as you cut through it. For a large chicken, separate the drumstick from the thigh by cutting through the knee joint.

To remove the wings, using the wishbone as a guide, cut diagonally through the shoulder joint. If the chicken is small, you can slip the breast meat off the breastbone in one piece. For a larger breast, cut thick slices downward from the breastbone. Alternatively, you can cut thinner slices, keeping them parallel to the breastbone.

BASTING DURING ROASTING

Spooning the cooking juices over a chicken during roasting prevents the bird from drying out. You can use a kitchen ladle or a bulb baster to do this. Remember the juices will be very hot so make sure you wear ovenproof gloves to protect your hands when basting.

Other Cooking Methods

Grilling, barbecuing, poaching, frying and stir-frying are some of the other methods that can be used to cook chicken.

Instead of roasting a chicken, many recipes call for frying or sautéing. Sometimes chicken is partially cooked by frying before being baked in a dish in the oven. This technique is used to brown the skin, giving it some colour, and adds flavour to the dish. Leaving the skin on will prevent the meat from drying out. A medium-low heat under the pan will melt the fat under the skin, while a high heat will brown the skin but not allow enough time for the fat to melt away.

BROWNING OR SAUTÉING

■ Before cooking, let the meat come to room temperature – it will absorb less fat.
■ Pat the chicken dry with kitchen paper so that the meat browns more quickly.
■ Cut the chicken into evenly sized chunks.
■ Make sure there is room in the pan for the pieces to brown evenly. If not, cook the chicken chunks in batches.

A NO-FAT OPTION

One way to cook chicken without adding any fat is by poaching it. This is where chicken is cooked in a pan of simmering water. A younger bird will need less poaching than an older one, which should be poached until the meat begins to fall away from the bone. Chicken portions can be poached, too.

BARBECUING

Chicken is a favourite for summertime barbecues.

■ When barbecuing over coals, make sure they are hot before you start cooking. Coals that are ready will look an ashy grey colour on the outside, while glowing red on the inside.

■ While a gas or electric barbecue will have knobs to adjust the temperature, you'll need to lower or raise the grill to adjust the heat over a barbecue that's fuelled by briquettes.

■ If you use wooden or bamboo skewers for kebabs, soak them in water for 30 minutes beforehand to prevent scorching.

GRILLING

You can cook a small chicken such as a poussin whole under the grill – it is often cut in half or spatchcocked first.

■ Always make sure the grill has been preheated so that it is very hot before grilling chicken.

■ Because chicken is prone to drying out under the grill, it is necessary to baste it regularly as it cooks – you can use melted butter or oil. A marinade made with oil is ideal for this and will add flavour, too.

■ It is important that the meat is cooked all the way through, so poach any thicker portions before grilling it. This also applies to chicken that will be barbecued.

MARINADES are a great way to add flavour or tenderize chicken as well as helping to prevent meat drying out during cooking.

■ Mix marinade ingredients in a non-metallic bowl as metal reacts with the acid in vinegar, wine and lemon juice.

■ You can also put the chicken in a sealable plastic bag with the marinade.

■ Acid ingredients in marinades (eg, lemon juice, vinegar and wine) break down and tenderize meat.

■ Oil-based marinades are great for adding flavour and locking in moisture. Oils infused with other ingredients, such as chillies, garlic and herbs give a more intense flavour to the marinated meat.

■ Keep marinating chicken covered in the fridge to avoid any bacterial growth.

■ The average time for marinating chicken is 2–4 hours (see recipe for exact ingredients and marinade timings).

Store-cupboard Essentials

Depending on the types of chicken recipes you prefer, there are some ingredients that you should always keep in stock.

Having the essential ingredients in your store cupboard will make it easy for you to prepare a chicken-based dish at short notice, so you'll need only a few ingredients from the shop. Basic ingredients that you should always have to hand include:

- a vegetable oil;
- olive oil;
- cornflour;
- rice;
- couscous/pasta/noodles.

Other stock ingredients depend on the types of food you like to cook:

- Oriental – soy sauce, groundnut oil, sesame oil, rice vinegar and rice wine;
- Curries – curry pastes and sauces, coconut milk or cream;
- Italian – canned tomatoes and pulses;
- Mexican – canned kidney beans, chilli powder, cumin, dried chillies.

Marinades are popular for barbecues and grilled chicken because they make the meat more succulent and come in a huge range with a variety of flavours.

HERBS AND SPICES FOR CHICKEN
Certain herbs and spices go well with chicken and keeping dried versions in your cupboard will mean you'll have plenty of choices for seasoning your dish. Some recommendations are:
- basil ■ bay leaf ■ coriander ■ garlic ■ ginger ■ majoram
- oregano ■ rosemary ■ sage ■ tarragon ■ thyme

Tinned tomatoes and pulses will be handy for Italian dishes.

FLAVOURING THE SKIN Here's how to add a flavoured butter under the chicken skin.

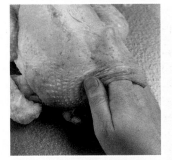

1 Pull back the skin at one side of the neck and push your fingers under the skin. Carefully work your fingers further under the skin so that you pull the skin away from the flesh. Repeat on the other side of the breast.

2 Scoop up some flavoured butter with your hand and push it under the skin. Still using your fingers, push the butter right under the skin so that the meat is completely covered. Repeat on the other side.

FLAVOURED BUTTER
A great way to flavour or moisten the meat of chicken and turkey is to push some butter and flavourings under the breast skin. Use softened butter mixed with herbs, spices or flavourings such as grated lemon zest or mashed anchovies.

Chicken Stock

A stock made from chicken bones and vegetables is one of the most versatile and useful ingredients. Here's how to get it just right.

The very best chicken stock is home made. You can make it ahead of time and refrigerate until needed. However, store-bought ready-made stock is a handy alternative. It will have better flavouring than stock cubes, although these are a useful back-up.

A SUCCESSFUL STOCK

- Always use cold water. This will avoid melting the fat too soon, so the stock is less likely to be cloudy.
- Simmer slowly. Let the water come to the boil slowly, then turn the heat down to a gentle simmer.
- Skim off any foaming scum. Do this as the stock comes to the boil and from time to time to keep the stock clear.
- Never cover the pot. Some liquid is meant to evaporate so that the stock gains a concentrated flavour.
- Strain the hot stock carefully through a sieve into a clean container to remove stray bits of flesh or bone.
- Allow to cool, preferably overnight in the fridge, and scrape off the set fat with a spoon. However, if the stock is needed straight away, drag a sheet of kitchen paper over the surface of the strained hot stock to pick up any blobs of fat.
- In a sealed container, a stock will keep for 3–4 days in the fridge or up to 2 months in the freezer. If you make a large batch, freeze the stock in useable portions.

MAKING CHICKEN STOCK

Makes about 1.2 litres (2 pints)

- **900g (2lb) raw chicken carcasses (eg, chicken wing bargain packs)**
- **25g (1oz) unsalted butter**
- **1 onion, peeled and chopped**
- **1 celery stick, chopped**
- **1 leek, cleaned and roughly chopped**
- **3 black peppercorns**
- **1 bay leaf**
- **1 sprig of fresh thyme**
- **1.8–2.1 litres (3–3½ pints) cold water**

1 In a large saucepan, melt the butter and soften the onion, celery and leek. Add the chicken, peppercorns, bay leaf and thyme.

2 Cover with the water and bring slowly to the boil. With a metal spoon, skim off any scum that rises to the surface. Reduce the heat and simmer for 2–3 hours.

3 Strain the stock through a sieve set over a large bowl. Throw away the bones, herbs and vegetables.

4 Leave the strained stock to cool before putting it in the fridge or freezer until needed.

21

Nibbles & Starters

Chicken Satay Skewers

Party Snack

TRY THIS...
with warm naan bread and extra satay sauce for dipping.

PREP TIME 5 MINS **COOK TIME** 10–12 MINS

- 2 chicken breasts, thinly sliced
- 4 teaspoons crunchy peanut butter
- 1 teaspoon chilli powder
- 2 tablespoons soy sauce

FOR THE CHUNKY SALAD

- ½ onion, peeled and finely sliced
- 2 small carrots, cut into sticks
- ½ small cabbage, shredded
- grated rind and juice of 1 lime
- 1 tablespoon olive oil
- 1 tablespoon fresh coriander, chopped
- salt and freshly ground black pepper

1 Put the peanut butter in a small saucepan with the chilli powder, soy sauce and about 200ml (7fl oz) hot water. Stir over a gentle heat until combined.

2 Thread the chicken onto 8 small bamboo skewers and brush generously with the satay mixture. Cook under a hot grill for 8–10 minutes, turning occasionally.

3 Meanwhile, make the salad. Put the onion, carrots and cabbage in a bowl and drizzle over the olive oil, lime rind and juice. Season and mix together well. Place the satay skewers on top.

! CONTAINS NUTS

SERVES 4 PER SERVING 232 CALS 12g FAT

Lemon Chicken Soup

Tasty Starter

PREP TIME 5 MINS **COOK TIME** 27 MINS

**!
CONTAINS
NUTS**

- 2 chicken breasts, with skin on
- 600ml (1 pint) ready-made or home-made chicken stock
- 1 carrot, peeled and diced
- 1 stick celery, diced
- 2 tablespoons basmati or long-grain rice
- ½ lemon, zest and 2 tablespoons juice
- 2 spring onions, trimmed, washed and finely sliced
- 2 tablespoons parsley, chopped
- salt and freshly ground black pepper
- 1 tablespoon almond flakes, toasted

1 Pour the stock into a large saucepan. Bring to the boil and add the carrot, celery and the rice. Reduce the heat to low and leave to simmer for 10 minutes.

2 Add the chicken and simmer for 15 minutes, then check that the rice and vegetables are just cooked. Remove the chicken, cut off the skin and cut the meat into strips.

3 Stir the lemon zest and juice into the soup, add the spring onions and half of the parsley and season to taste.

4 Divide the strips of meat between two warmed soup bowls and then spoon the soup over the top. Sprinkle with the rest of the parsley and the almonds.

CHEF'S TIP
Good home-made stock really makes a difference to a soup, so it is definitely worth the effort. Stock freezes for up to 2 months.

SERVES 2 PER SERVING 297 CALS 4g FAT

Spicy Chicken Wings & BBQ Beans

Lunchtime Snack

PREP TIME 15 MINS **COOK TIME** 20 MINS

- 12 large chicken wings
- 1 clove garlic, peeled and crushed
- 3 tablespoons white wine vinegar
- 6 tablespoons soy sauce
- 1 tablespoon tomato purée
- 1 teaspoon English mustard
- 1 tablespoon brown sugar
- 820g canned baked beans
- fries, to serve
- lemon wedges, to garnish

1 Preheat the oven to 200°C/400°F/Gas 6. Combine the garlic, vinegar, soy sauce, purée, mustard and sugar in a small bowl.

2 Put the wings in a roasting pan and pour over the sauce, reserving 2 tablespoons. Bake for 20–25 minutes. Heat the baked beans and stir in the remaining barbeque sauce. Serve the chicken wings and beans with fries and garnish with lemon wedges.

CHEF'S TIP
Remember to oil the roasting pan lightly to avoid the chicken wings sticking to the pan during cooking.

LOW IN FAT

SERVES 4 PER SERVING 255 CALS 3g FAT

Chargrilled Chicken & Salsa Waffle Stacks

Light Supper

PREP TIME 10 MINS **COOK TIME** 15 MINS

- **4 chicken breasts, skinless**
- **8 potato waffles**
- **juice of 1 lime**
- **½ small red onion, very finely chopped**
- **150g (5oz) cherry tomatoes, quartered**
- **1 tablespoon fresh coriander, chopped**
- **salt and freshly ground black pepper**
- **1 avocado, peeled and sliced**

1 Cook the waffles according to the pack instructions. Cut each chicken breast in half horizontally and squeeze half the lime juice over them. Season and cook for 2–3 minutes on each side in a preheated griddle pan.

2 To make the salsa, mix 2 teaspoons lime juice with the chopped red onion, then stir in the cherry tomatoes, coriander and seasoning.

3 For each person, layer 2 waffles with a quarter of the sliced avocado and 2 pieces of chicken. Spoon over the salsa and serve with mangetout and baby sweetcorn.

SERVES 4 PER SERVING 424 CALS 18.8g FAT

Southern-style Chicken & Chips

Weekday Dinner

PREP TIME 15 MINS **COOK TIME** 35 MINS

- 4 chicken quarters, skinned
- 2 baking potatoes, scrubbed
- 2 sweet potatoes, peeled
- a few bursts spray oil
- 1½ teaspoons hot smoked paprika
- 1½ teaspoons dried onion granules
- 1½ teaspoons dried thyme
- 2 tablespoons plain flour
- salt and freshly ground black pepper
- 1 egg, beaten
- 6 tablespoons dry white breadcrumbs
- 1 tablespoon fresh thyme, chopped
- tomato ketchup, to serve

CHEF'S TIP
Delicious with a crisp coleslaw salad tossed in a light mayonnaise and fromage frais dressing.

1 Preheat the oven to 220°C/425°F/Gas 7. Cut baking and sweet potatoes into lengthwise chips about 1cm (½in) thick. Line two baking sheets with baking parchment and arrange the chips evenly and well spaced out on the top of one of them. Spray lightly with oil.

2 Mix together 1 teaspoon each of paprika, onion granules and dried thyme and sprinkle over the chips. Season to taste and bake for 30–35 minutes until tender, crisp and golden.

3 Meanwhile, wash and pat dry the chicken. Mix the flour with the remaining paprika, onion granules and dried thyme, and season. Dust the chicken all over with the mixture.

4 On a plate, beat the egg with 2 tablespoons water. Place the breadcrumbs on another plate. Dip the chicken first in egg and then in breadcrumbs to coat evenly. Place on a second prepared baking sheet. Spray with oil and bake for 30 minutes, or until cooked through.

5 Pile the chips on a warm serving plate and sprinkle with fresh thyme. Top with a piece of chicken and serve with tomato ketchup.

SERVES 4 PER SERVING 483 CALS 7g FAT

Oriental Chicken Noodle Soup

Quick Soup

PREP TIME 5 MINS **COOK TIME** 5 MINS

- 200g pack cooked chicken mini fillets, sliced
- 2 chicken stock cubes
- 4 tablespoons medium or dry sherry
- 1 tablespoon soy sauce
- 410g canned baby sweetcorn, drained and sliced
- 300g (11oz) fine wok noodles
- 4 spring onions, sliced

1 Make the chicken stock cubes up to 1.2 litres (2 pints) with boiling water in a large pan. Add the remaining ingredients and heat through for 3–4 minutes. Ladle into bowls and serve immediately.

LOW IN FAT

SERVES 4 **PER SERVING 253** CALS **3.9g** FAT

Glazed Chicken Drumsticks

Family Tea-time

PREP TIME 5 MINS **COOK TIME** 30–35 MINS

- **1kg (2lb 4oz) chicken thighs and drumsticks**
- **6 tablespoons tomato ketchup**
- **6 tablespoons mango chutney**
- **1 teaspoon garlic purée**
- **juice of ½ lemon**
- **½ teaspoon hot red pepper sauce**
- **rice salad, to serve**

1 Preheat the oven to 200°C/400°F/Gas 6. Whisk together the ketchup, chutney, garlic purée, lemon juice and hot red pepper sauce Pour over the chicken pieces in a roasting tin.

2 Roast the chicken for 30–35 minutes or until the juices run clear when the thigh is pierced with a small knife. Brush the chicken with the sauce once or twice during cooking. Serve with rice salad.

TRY THIS... without the hot red pepper sauce for children's teas.

SERVES 4 PER SERVING 614 CALS 37g FAT

Chicken Nachos

Weekday Supper

PREP TIME 5 MINS **COOK TIME** 5 MINS

- 2 cooked chicken breast fillets, roughly chopped
- 200g tortilla chips
- 410g canned mixed pulses, drained and rinsed
- 1 avocado, peeled and sliced
- ½ red onion, peeled and sliced
- 300g ready-made salsa
- 125g (4oz) Cheddar cheese, grated

1 Layer up the tortilla chips with the pulses, chicken, avocado, red onion and salsa in a shallow, heatproof serving dish. Scatter the cheese over the top and place under a medium grill until the cheese has melted. Serve immediately.

TRY THIS...
with extra tortilla chips on the side.

SERVES 4 PER SERVING 608 CALS 29.5g FAT

Fruity Coronation Chicken

Weekday Supper

PREP TIME 10 MINS **COOK TIME** 10 MINS

- 500g (18oz) cooked chicken, skinned
- 4 ripe peaches, peeled
- 4 tablespoons low-fat fromage frais
- 2 tablespoons low-calorie mayonnaise
- 2 teaspoons mild curry paste
- 1 tablespoon spicy mango chutney
- salt and freshly ground black pepper
- a few sprigs fresh coriander
- 125g (4oz) assorted salad leaves
- 15g (½oz) flaked almonds, toasted

1 Cut the chicken into bite-sized pieces and place in a bowl. Wash and pat dry the peaches, then halve them and remove the stones. Slice into thin wedges.

2 Mix together the fromage frais, mayo, curry paste, chutney and seasoning. Carefully stir into the cooked chicken along with the peaches until well mixed.

3 Mix the coriander and salad leaves and put onto a serving dish. Top with the chicken and sprinkle with the flaked almonds.

! CONTAINS NUTS

LOW IN FAT

SERVES 4 PER SERVING 226 CALS 6.3g FAT

Pesto Chicken

PREP TIME 10 MINS **COOK TIME** 40 MINS

Light Bite

- 4 chicken breasts, skinned and cut into strips
- a few sprays olive oil
- 4 tablespoons crème fraîche

FOR THE PESTO
- 50g (2oz) flat-leaved parsley
- 8 halves or 15g roughly chopped walnuts
- 5 tablespoons olive oil
- 1 clove garlic, peeled and chopped
- ½ teaspoon salt
- 3 tablespoons Parmesan cheese, freshly grated

1 First prepare the pesto. Wash the parsley and dry it gently. Heat a non-stick frying pan and dry-fry the walnuts until lightly toasted. Put them in a small food processor with the garlic, salt and parsley. Pulse a few times. Add the cheese and olive oil. Whizz again once to blend.

2 Heat a little oil in a wok or large frying pan and add the chicken strips in one layer. Cook for 2–3 minutes until the strips are brown then turn over and cook for another couple of minutes.

3 Add the crème fraîche and 3 tablespoons of the pesto and simmer for 5 minutes. Add 2 tablespoons more of pesto, mix and serve.

TRY THIS...
with roast potatoes
and a small dish
of extra pesto for
dipping.

SERVES 4 PER SERVING 382 CALS **27.1g** FAT

! CONTAINS NUTS

Peanut Chicken Kebabs

Great Starter

PREP TIME 15 MINS + MARINATING
COOK TIME 20 MINS

- 2 chicken breasts, skinned
- 8 cherry tomatoes
- 1 red onion, peeled, quartered and split into pieces
- 1 yellow pepper, deseeded and cut into pieces

FOR THE MARINADE

- 2 tablespoons crunchy peanut butter
- 5 tablespoons soured cream
- 150g (5oz) low-fat fromage frais
- 1 tablespoon lemon juice
- 1 clove garlic, peeled and crushed
- ½ teaspoon grated root ginger
- 1 teaspoon light soy sauce
- 1 teaspoon ground coriander
- few drops of hot red pepper sauce

1 Cut the chicken into 2cm cubes and place in a shallow dish. Combine all the marinade ingredients together. Spoon the marinade over the chicken and stir well. Cover and chill for 4–6 hours, stirring occasionally.

2 Thread the chicken, tomatoes, onion and pepper onto four skewers. Baste with the marinade and cook under a moderate grill or on a barbecue for 15–20 minutes, turning frequently and brushing with marinade, until thoroughly cooked.

224 CALS PER SERVING

! CONTAINS NUTS

SERVES 4 PER SERVING **224** CALS **16.1g** FAT

Tzatziki Chicken

Tasty Snack

TRY THIS...
with a tomato salad and strips of pitta bread.

PREP TIME	10 MINS + MARINATING
COOK TIME	15 MINS

- 8 chicken thigh fillets
- 300ml (½ pint) reduced-fat Greek yoghurt
- 2 tablespoons fresh mint, chopped
- 1 teaspoon dried mint
- 2 cloves garlic, peeled and crushed

FOR THE TZATZIKI
- ½ cucumber, deseeded and diced
- salt and freshly ground black pepper

1 Mix the yoghurt with the fresh and dried mint and garlic. Transfer half to a bowl, cover and chill. Place the remainder in a dish, add the chicken thigh fillets and turn to coat in the mixture. Cover and leave to marinate for 4 hours.

2 Cook the chicken fillets for 7–8 minutes each side under a preheated grill, or on a griddle pan over a medium heat. The chicken juices should run clear when the thickest part is pierced with a sharp knife.

3 Mix the reserved yoghurt with the diced cucumber and seasoning to make the tzatziki. Serve with the grilled chicken thighs.

SERVES 4 PER SERVING 259 CALS 11.1g FAT

Chicken Caesar Kebabs

Light Bite

PREP TIME 5 MINS + MARINATING
COOK TIME 12–15 MINS

- 4 chicken breasts, diced
- 5 tablespoons Caesar salad dressing
- 2 courgettes, cut into chunks
- 1 bunch spring onions, cut into thirds

1 Marinate the chicken in half the Caesar dressing for 20 minutes. Thread onto soaked bamboo skewers with the chunks of courgette and spring onions.

2 Grill for 12–15 minutes, turning regularly, until cooked through. Drizzle with the remaining Caesar dressing.

TRY THIS...
with a large green salad or with herbed rice on the side.

SERVES 4 PER SERVING **237** CALS **10.3g** FAT

Sticky Chicken with Mango Salsa

Family Tea-time

PREP TIME	15 MINS + MARINATING
COOK TIME	10 MINS

- 4 chicken breasts, skinned
- 2 limes, juice from both, zest from 1
- 1 or 2 garlic cloves, peeled and crushed
- 2 teaspoons olive oil
- 2 tablespoons honey
- 1 tablespoons tomato ketchup
- 1 teaspoon soy sauce
- 1 teaspoon wholegrain mustard

FOR THE SALSA

- 1 small red onion, peeled and diced
- 1 mango, stoned, peeled and diced
- 8 cherry tomatoes, chopped

1 Cut the chicken into thin strips. Mix the juice from 1 lime with the crushed garlic in a shallow dish. Coat the chicken strips and leave to marinate for at least 20 minutes.

2 Heat the oil in a large non-stick frying pan. Remove the chicken from the marinade. Put in the pan and cook over a medium heat for 2 minutes on each side. Remove from heat.

3 Mix the honey, ketchup, soy sauce and mustard in a bowl. Brush over the chicken in the pan on both sides. Return pan to a low heat and cook for 3 minutes on each side.

4 Make the salsa by mixing the onion, zest and juice from the remaining lime, diced mango and chopped tomatoes in a bowl. Serve the chicken with a large spoonful of salsa.

CHEF'S TIP

Don't have the heat too high after the glaze goes on or it may burn. You can pour any glaze left in the pan over the cooked chicken.

LOW IN FAT

SERVES 4 PER SERVING 328 CALS 4g FAT

Baked & Roasted

Pot Roast Chicken on Braised Root Veg

Family Favourite

PREP TIME 2 MINS **COOK TIME** 70 MINS

- 1 chicken approx 1.25kg (2lb 13oz)
- 1 tablespoon sunflower oil
- 300ml (½ pint) chicken stock
- a few sprigs of fresh thyme
- 10 cloves of garlic, peeled
- 250g (9oz) frozen casserole vegetables

1 Preheat the oven to 200°C/400°F/Gas 6. In a deep, flameproof casserole, brown the chicken in the oil. Add the stock, thyme, garlic and seasoning, bring to a simmer and cover the casserole tightly with a lid or foil.

2 Place in the oven and cook for 45 minutes, then add the vegetables, pushing them down into the liquid. Cook for a further 15 minutes and serve.

CHEF'S TIP
You can use just water if you don't have a stock cube. Why not use the chicken's carcass to make some home-made stock?

SERVES 4 PER SERVING 501 CALS 29.1g FAT

Honey & Lemon Chicken Breasts

Tasty Dinner

PREP TIME 5 MINS **COOK TIME** 25 MINS

- **4 chicken breasts, skinless**
- **1 lemon**
- **2 tablespoons clear honey**
- **1 tablespoon grain mustard**
- **1 tablespoon olive oil**
- **salt and freshly ground black pepper**

1 Preheat the oven to 180°C/350°F/Gas 4 and line a roasting tin with a large piece of overhanging foil. Place the chicken breasts in the tin. Cut 4 thin slices from the lemon and place one on top of each chicken breast.

2 Squeeze the juice from the lemon and mix with the honey, mustard, oil and seasoning, then drizzle over the chicken. Seal the foil.

3 Bake for 15 minutes, fold back the foil and baste. Cook uncovered for 10 minutes more.

TRY THIS... with vegetables and potatoes, such as mash and baby veg.

LOW IN FAT

SERVES 4 PER SERVING 212 CALS 5.2g FAT

Stuffed Chicken Breasts

PREP TIME 10 MINS **COOK TIME** 25 MINS

Dinner Party Idea

- 5 small chicken breasts, skinned
- 1 tablespoon whipping cream,
- 1 tablespoon Parmesan cheese, grated
- 2–3 tablespoons toasted hazelnuts
- 50g (2oz) sun-dried tomatoes, drained
- salt and freshly ground black pepper
- 8 slices Parma ham

FOR THE SAUCE
- 1 teaspoon flour
- 200ml (7fl oz) whipping cream
- 1 tablespoon nutmeg, grated
- 1 tablespoon toasted hazlenuts

1 Preheat the oven to 180°C/350°F/Gas 4. Take one of the chicken breasts, chop it roughly and put into the food processor. Add the cream, Parmesan, hazelnuts and sun-dried tomatoes and blend. Season well.

2 Slice open the remaining chicken breasts. Form the chicken mince into 4 sausage shapes. Lay each sausage on a breast and wrap the meat around it. Wrap each chicken breast in 2 slices of Parma ham and arrange on a baking sheet. Bake for 25 minutes.

3 To make the sauce, whisk the flour into the cream in a saucepan and heat slowly, whisking until thickened. Season with salt, pepper and nutmeg. Add the hazelnuts. Slice the chicken rolls and serve with the sauce.

!
CONTAINS NUTS

CHEF'S TIP
To toast the hazelnuts, put on a baking tray in a hot oven for 5 minutes. Allow to cool a little before rubbing off the skins.

SERVES 4 **PER SERVING 511** CALS **35.8g** FAT

Italian Chicken & Pasta

Quick Supper

- ■ **4 chicken breasts, skinless and boneless**
- ■ **220g jar sun-dried tomatoes, chopped**
- ■ **200g tub mini mozzarella balls**
- ■ **handful of fresh basil leaves, torn**
- ■ **1 tablespoon extra virgin olive oil**
- ■ **salt and ground black pepper**
- ■ **cooked pasta, to serve**

1 Preheat oven to 190°C/373°F/Gas 5. Score 4 deep slashes on top of each chicken breast, about 2cm (1in) deep. Fill each slash with some of the sun-dried tomatoes, mozzarella balls and basil leaves.

2 Place the chicken breasts on a baking tray, then drizzle over the olive oil, season and bake for 20 minutes, until cooked through.

3 Serve with cooked pasta and garnish with the remaining sun-dried tomatoes, mozzarella balls and basil leaves.

SERVES 4 PER SERVING 387 CALS 22.5g FAT

Oven-baked Lemony Chicken & Rice

Family Supper

PREP TIME 10 MINS **COOK TIME** 45 MINS

- 4 chicken breasts, with skin on
- 2 tablespoons olive oil
- 4 spring onions, sliced
- 2 garlic cloves, finely chopped
- 250g (9oz) long-grain rice
- 1 lemon, sliced
- 600ml (1 pint) chicken stock
- salt and freshly ground black pepper
- 2 tablespoons fresh tarragon, chopped
- 1 tablespoon pine nuts, toasted

1 Preheat the oven to 190°C /375°F/Gas 5. Heat the oil in a medium-sized roasting tin on the hob and fry the chicken breasts skin-side down for 4–5 minutes, until browned. Turn the chicken over and cook for a further 1–2 minutes. Remove from the pan and keep warm.

2 Add the spring onions and garlic to the pan and cook gently for 2–3 minutes until softened. Stir in the rice and lemon slices and pour in the stock. Mix well and season with salt and freshly ground pepper. Place the chicken breasts on top of the rice mixture.

3 Cover carefully with foil and bake in the oven for 30–35 minutes until all the stock has been absorbed and the rice is tender. Stir in the tarragon and pine nuts and serve straight away.

SERVES 4 PER SERVING 575 CALS 24.3g FAT

Chicken, Mushroom, & Leek Puff Pie

Hearty Dinner

PREP TIME 15 MINS + COOL & CHILL
COOK TIME 25 MINS

CHEF'S TIP
Four individual pie dishes or heatproof serving bowls can be used. Leave a gap of 5mm below rim of dish and the top of filling.

- 2 large chicken breasts, skinless and chopped into large pieces
- 25g (1oz) butter, chopped into cubes
- 2 leeks, washed and finely sliced
- 2 tablespoons fresh thyme leaves
- 225g (8oz) mushrooms, sliced
- 1 garlic clove, crushed
- 200g (7oz) cream cheese
- 275g (10oz) ready-rolled puff pastry
- 1 egg, beaten with a pinch of salt

1 Preheat the oven to 220°C /425°F/Gas 7. Heat half the butter in a large frying pan until melted. Add the chicken, leeks and thyme and fry for 5–8 minutes. Transfer to a bowl.

2 Melt the remaining butter and add the mushrooms and garlic. Cook for 5 minutes. Remove from the heat, add the leeks and chicken and season well. Cover and allow to cool. Add the cream cheese and mix well. Spoon the filling into a large pie dish with a lip.

3 On a floured surface, roll out the puff pastry to a thickness of about 5mm (¼in). Cut a long strip of pastry and fix to the pie dish edge with a little egg. Brush rim with the beaten egg and lift the pie lid on top. Press the edges together. Chill in the fridge for 15 minutes.

4 Brush pastry top with remaining egg and place in oven for 25 minutes or until the pastry has risen and is golden brown .

SERVES 4 PER SERVING 654 CALS 41.5g FAT

Chicken & Fennel Pasta Bake

Lunchtime Meal

PREP TIME 15 MINS **COOK TIME** 40 MINS

- 225g (8oz) chicken breasts, cooked and chopped
- 2 red onions, peeled and finely sliced
- 1 tablespoon lemon juice
- 2 teaspoons olive oil
- 2 fennel bulbs, trimmed and sliced
- salt and freshly ground black pepper
- 225g (8oz) pasta, eg penne
- 50g (2oz) sultanas
- 400g (14oz) light cream cheese with garlic and chives
- 4 tablespoons milk
- 2 tablespoons chives, chopped
- 1 teaspoon grated lemon zest
- 75g (3oz) low-fat mozzarella, drained and thinly sliced

1 Preheat the oven to 200°C/400°F/Gas 6. Toss the red onions in the lemon juice. Heat the oil in a large frying pan and gently fry the fennel and onion for 4–5 minutes, stirring, until beginning to soften. Transfer to a heatproof bowl, season to taste and set aside.

2 Bring a large saucepan of water to the boil and cook the pasta according to the instructions until just cooked. Drain well and toss into the vegetables.

3 Add the chicken to the pasta along with the sultanas. Mix together the cheese and milk and stir into the pasta along with the chives and lemon zest.

4 Mix well and then pile into an ovenproof baking dish and place on a baking sheet. Arrange the mozzarella on top and bake in the oven for 20–25 minutes until golden.

TRY THIS...
with a large
rocket salad on
the side.

SERVES 4 PER SERVING 577 CALS 23g FAT

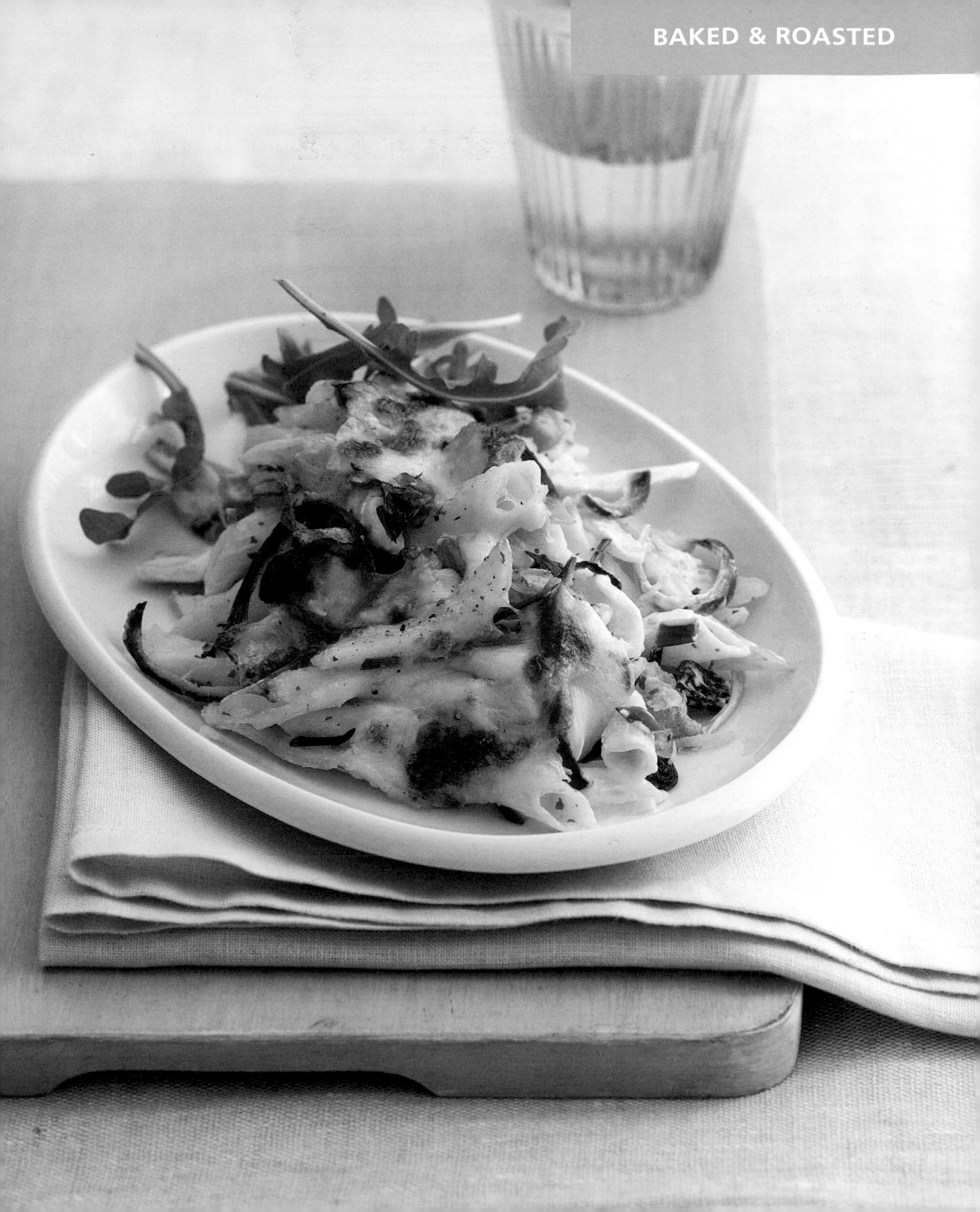

Creamy Chicken Breasts

Easy Meal

PREP TIME 10 MINS **COOK TIME** 30 MINS

- ■ 4 chicken breasts, skinless
- ■ 4 tablespoons light garlic-and-herbs cream cheese
- ■ 8 rashers streaky bacon
- ■ 300g (11oz) cherry tomatoes (preferably on the vine)
- ■ 1 tablespoon dried thyme
- ■ low-fat cooking spray

1 Preheat the oven to 200°C/400°F/Gas 6. Cut a pocket in each chicken breast using a small, sharp knife, then stuff 1 tablespoon of the light cream cheese into each one.

2 Wrap 2 rashers of bacon around each stuffed chicken breast and place In a roasting tin. Spritz with low-fat cooking spray and roast for 20 minutes.

3 Add the tomatoes to the roasting tin, then lightly coat with more low-fat cooking spray and sprinkle the thyme all over. Roast for a further 8 minutes or until the chicken is thoroughly cooked through.

SERVES 4 PER SERVING 285 CALS 12.5g FAT

Italian Stuffed Chicken

PREP TIME 15 MINS **COOK TIME** 25 MINS

Dinner Party Idea

- 4 chicken breast fillets, skinless
- 50g (2oz) sun-dried tomatoes, chopped
- 200g (7oz) ricotta cheese
- 15g (½oz) fresh basil leaves, roughly torn
- salt and freshly ground black pepper
- 8 slices of Parma ham
- roasted vegetables, to serve

1 Preheat the oven to 190°C/375°F/Gas 5. Mix together the sun-dried tomatoes, ricotta and basil (saving a few leaves to garnish) in a bowl and season.

2 Cut a horizontal slit in the side of each chicken breast. Fill with the ricotta mixture. Wrap each breast with two strips of Parma ham so that the joins are underneath and fix in place with cocktail sticks.

3 Put the stuffed chicken breasts on a baking tray and bake for 20–25 minutes or until golden and cooked through.

4 Remove the cocktail sticks and slice in half. Serve with roasted vegetables and garnish with basil leaves.

LOW IN FAT

SERVES 4 PER SERVING 288 CALS 8.5g FAT

Cheesy Chicken & Leek Gratin

Weekday Supper

PREP TIME 15 MINS **COOK TIME** 20 MINS

- 1 chicken breast, skinless
- 1 tablespoon vegetable oil
- 2 leeks, trimmed, washed and sliced
- 300ml (½ pint) ready-made white sauce
- 2 tablespoons fresh chives, snipped
- salt and freshly ground black pepper
- 1 French baton-style roll, thinly sliced
- 1 tablespoon wholegrain mustard
- 50g (2oz) Cheddar cheese, grated

1 Heat the oil in a large saucepan and gently fry the leeks for 5 minutes until they are softened but not browned. Stir the chicken, white sauce and chives into the leeks and season lightly. Heat gently, stirring, for about 5 minutes until piping hot and the chicken is cooked.

2 Preheat the grill to hot. Arrange the bread slices on the grill rack and toast until lightly brown. Transfer the chicken and leek sauce to a small, shallow, ovenproof dish.

3 Spread each of the toasted bread slices with mustard and then arrange on top of the chicken mixture, mustard-side up. Sprinkle with the cheese and place in the grill rack.

4 Cook under the grill for 3–4 minutes until the cheese is bubbling and golden on top. Serve immediately.

SERVES 2 PER SERVING 545 CALS 25g FAT

Italian Chicken Casserole

Hearty Dinner

PREP TIME 10 MINS **COOK TIME** 1 HOUR

- 1kg (2lb 4oz) chicken thighs and drumsticks
- 2 tablespoons olive oil
- 125g (4oz) bacon bits
- 150g (5oz) closed-cup mushrooms, quartered
- 500g jar tomato pasta sauce
- 1kg (2lb 4oz) potatoes, peeled and diced
- salt and freshly ground black pepper
- 1 tablespoon fresh rosemary, chopped
- 1 red onion, peeled and roughly chopped

1 Preheat the oven to 200°C/400°F/Gas 6. Heat 1 tablespoon of the oil in a flameproof casserole, add the chicken and brown for 3–4 minutes. Remove the chicken and set aside. Add the bacon and mushrooms. Fry for 3 minutes.

2 Return the chicken to the casserole, pour in the sauce plus 100ml (3½fl oz) water and bring to the boil. Cover, reduce heat and simmer for 45 minutes, until the chicken is cooked.

3 Meanwhile, boil the diced potatoes in salted water for 5 minutes. Drain and toss with the remaining oil and seasoning. Spread out on a baking tray and roast for 25 minutes, turning halfway.

4 Toss the rosemary and red onion through the potatoes and roast for 5 minutes. Serve the casserole with the sautéed potatoes.

SERVES 4 PER SERVING 735 CALS 32g FAT

Lemon & Tarragon Chicken

Weekend Dish

PREP TIME 1O MINS **COOK TIME** 1 HOUR

- 4 large or 8 small chicken pieces (eg thighs)
- 1 head of garlic, separated into cloves, but not peeled
- 8 shallots, halved lengthways
- 1 large lemon, thinly sliced
- 4 tablespoons fresh tarragon, chopped
- 200ml (7fl oz) dry white wine
- 200ml (7fl oz) chicken stock
- 4 medium potatoes, peeled and thickly sliced
- 2 red peppers, deseeded and sliced
- olive oil, to drizzle
- salt and freshly ground black pepper

1 Preheat the oven to 220°C/425°F/Gas 7. In a large ovenproof dish, arrange the chicken in a single layer. Scatter around the garlic, shallots, lemon and tarragon.

2 Pour over the white wine and stock and carefully arrange the potatoes and peppers around the chicken. Drizzle liberally with olive oil and season well.

3 Cover and place in the preheated oven and cook for about 30 minutes, then remove the cover and cook for another 25–30 minutes or until the chicken is cooked through and the vegetables are tender. Remove from the oven and allow to rest for 5–10 minutes.

TRY THIS...
with fresh, crusty bread and a crisp green salad on the side.

SERVES 4 PER SERVING 765 CALS 42.1g FAT

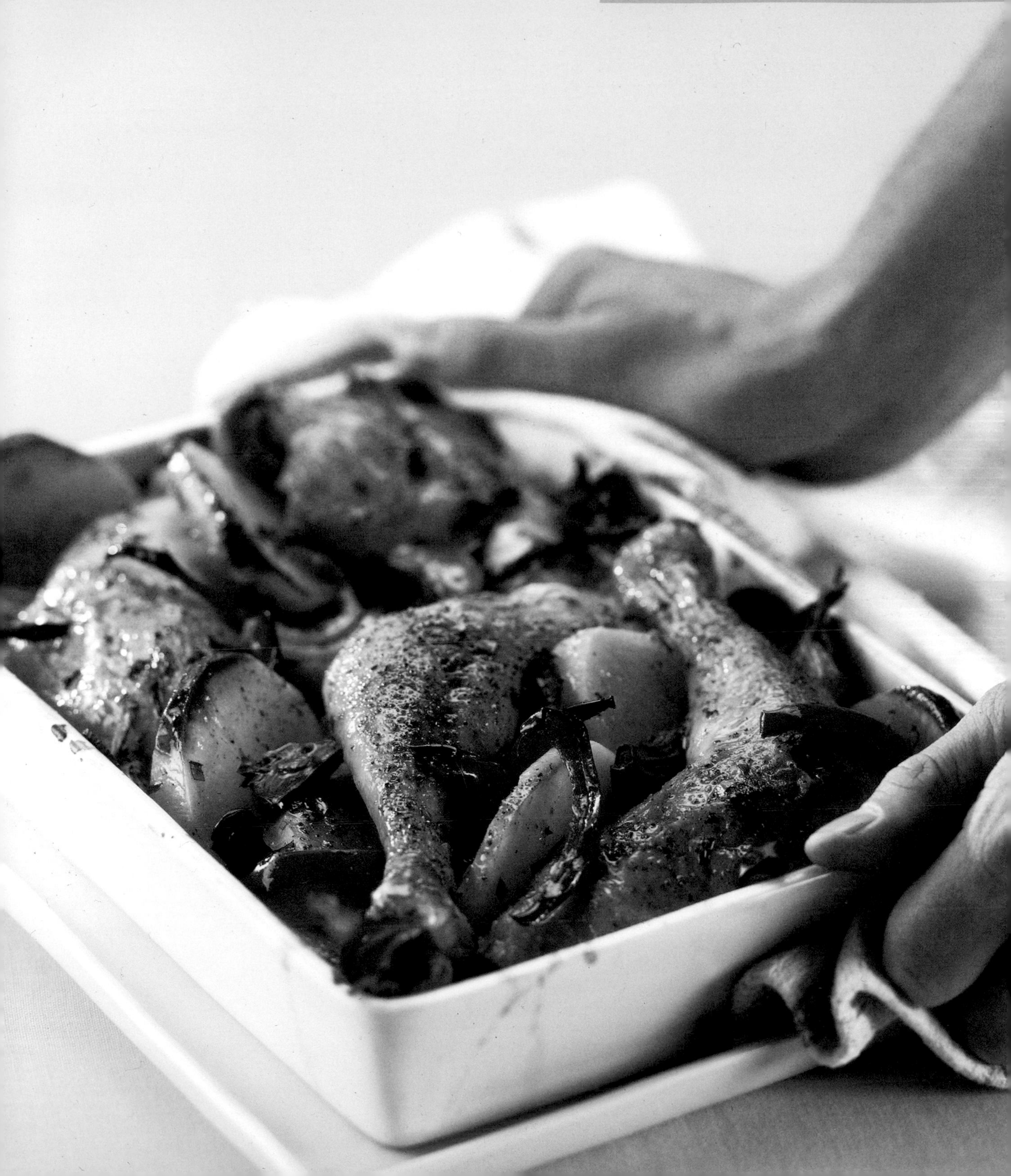

Brie-stuffed Chicken

Easy Meal

PREP TIME 5 MINS **COOK TIME** 20 MINS

- 4 chicken breasts, skinless boneless
- 200g pack garlic-and-herb flavoured Brie
- 8 bacon rashers, trimmed
- lemon thyme, to garnish
- cocktail sticks, to secure

1 Preheat oven to 190°C/375°F/Gas 5. Cut each chicken breast diagonally, then spread the middle of each with the Brie. Wrap 2 rashers of bacon around each chicken breast. Secure with a cocktail stick.

2 Place the wrapped chicken breasts on a baking tray and bake for 20 minutes, until chicken is cooked through. Garnish with lemon thyme.

TRY THIS... with potatoes and vegetables of your choice.

SERVES 4 PER SERVING 435 CALS 25.3g FAT

Soy Spatchcock Chicken

Family Favourite

PREP TIME 15 MINS + MARINATING
COOK TIME 80 MINS

- 1.25kg (2lb 13oz) chicken, spatchcocked
- juice of 1 lemon
- juice of 1 lime
- 50g (2oz) clear honey
- 2 tablespoons reduced salt soy sauce

1 To prepare the marinade, put the lemon and lime juice, honey and soy sauce into a large bowl and mix together well.

2 Ask your butcher to spatchcock the chicken for you. Put the chicken into the marinade and coat it well all over. Cover the bowl and refrigerate for 2–3 hours, or overnight if wished.

3 Heat the oven to 220°C/425°F/Gas 7. Place the chicken, opened out, in a roasting tin. Pour any remaining marinade over the chicken and add some water to the roasting tin so the honey juices don't burn. Cook in the centre of the oven for 30 minutes.

4 Reduce the heat to 180°C/350°F/Gas 4 and cook for another 30 minutes or until the chicken is cooked through, basting it frequently. Serve the chicken with new potatoes and a green salad or red cabbage.

LOW IN FAT

SERVES 4 PER SERVING **292** CALS **5.6g** FAT **SUITABLE FOR FREEZING**

All-in-One Lemony Roast Chicken

Family Favourite

PREP TIME 15 MINS **COOK TIME** 1 HOUR

- **4 chicken legs**
- **500g (18oz) baby new potatoes**
- **250g (9oz) baby carrots**
- **3 leeks, each cut into 6 chunks**
- **1 head garlic, separated into cloves and peeled**
- **2 tablespoons olive oil**
- **juice of 1 lemon**
- **1 tablespoon rosemary sprigs**

1 Preheat the oven to 220°C/425°F/Gas 7. Boil the new potatoes for 10–15 minutes until tender. Drain and toss with the carrots, leeks, garlic, chicken and the olive oil in a large roasting tin. Season and roast for 25 minutes.

2 Drizzle the lemon juice over the chicken and vegetables and mix in the rosemary. Return to the oven for 15 minutes until the chicken is cooked through. Serve immediately.

SERVES 4 PER SERVING 454 CALS 23g FAT

Chicken, Spinach & Cheese Roulades

Tasty Lunch

PREP TIME 10 MINS **COOK TIME** 15 MINS

TRY THIS... with roasted vine tomatoes on the side.

- 4 chicken breast fillets, skinless
- 100g (3½oz) light cream cheese with herbs and garlic
- 250g (9oz) frozen spinach, defrosted
- salt and freshly ground black pepper
- 1 tablespoon olive oil
- 350g (12oz) egg tagliatelle
- 2 teaspoons butter
- 3 tablespoons fresh mixed herbs, chopped
- cocktail sticks, to secure

1 Preheat the oven to 220°C/425°F/Gas 7. Cut the chicken breasts almost in half horizontally, then spread with cream cheese. Squeeze the excess liquid from the spinach and divide between the chicken breasts.

2 Season, then roll up like a swiss roll, starting from the pointed end. Secure each one with a cocktail stick and place in a roasting tin, then drizzle over half the olive oil. Roast for 15 minutes or until the juices from the chicken run clear when pierced.

3 Meanwhile cook the tagliatelle according to the instructions. Drain and toss with the butter and mixed herbs. Divide between 4 warmed bowls. Slice the chicken and arrange on the pasta.

SERVES 4 PER SERVING **599** CALS **11.8g** FAT

Salads & Light Meals

- Herby Chicken & Bacon Tortellini Salad

- Chicken Pasta with Stilton

- Chicken, Pineapple & Mango Kebabs

- Asian Chicken Salad

- Warm Chicken Caesar Salad

- Chicken & Mixed Vegetable Frittata

- Chicken Salad Niçoise

- Rice Noodle Salad

- Easy Chicken in Mustard Sauce

- Warm Mexican Chicken Salad

- Artichoke & Chicken Salad

- Chicken Quesadillas

- Herby Chicken Couscous

Herby Chicken & Bacon Tortellini Salad

Tasty Lunch

PREP TIME 5 MINS **COOK TIME** 15 MINS

- 2 chicken breasts, skinless
- 1 tablespoon olive oil
- 4 tablespoons fresh herbs, chopped
- 4 rashers streaky bacon
- 250g (9oz) filled, fresh tortellini
- 1 Romaine lettuce heart, leaves separated
- bread, to serve
- 2 tablespoons Caesar dressing, to serve

1 Preheat the oven to 200°C/400°F/Gas 6. Drizzle the oil over the chicken breasts and roll in the herbs to coat. Roast in the oven for 15 minutes or until cooked through. Allow to cool then slice.

2 Meanwhile, grill or fry the bacon until crisp, then crumble into small pieces. Simmer the tortellini in lightly salted water for 3 minutes, then drain and rinse in cold water.

3 Toss tortellini with the bacon and chicken. Serve with the Romaine leaves, Caesar dressing and bread.

SERVES 4 PER SERVING 757 CALS 33g FAT

Chicken Pasta with Stilton

Weekday Supper

PREP TIME 5 MINS **COOK TIME** 20 MINS

- 500g (18oz) chicken breasts, skinless
- 300g (11oz) pasta shapes
- 300g (11oz) broccoli, broken into florets
- 2 tablespoons olive oil
- 1 onion, peeled and chopped
- 175g (6oz) cherry tomatoes
- 150g (5oz) Stilton cheese
- 4 tablespoons double cream
- salt and freshly ground black pepper

1 Bring a saucepan of salted water to the boil, add the pasta and cook according to the instructions. For the last 5 minutes of the pasta cooking time, steam the broccoli over the pan. Drain the pasta and return to the pan. Toss in the broccoli and set aside.

2 Meanwhile, slice the chicken into thin strips. Heat the oil in a large frying pan and fry the onion and chicken strips for 7–8 minutes, stirring, until golden and cooked through.

3 Halve the cherry tomatoes and add to the pan. Cook gently for 1 minute. Crumble in the Stilton cheese and add the cream. Heat through, stirring, for 1 minute until melted.

4 Finally, add the chicken and the blue cheese mixture to the pasta and broccoli and stir well to mix. Heat through gently for 1–2 minutes until hot. Adjust seasoning to serve.

CHEF'S TIP
Use low-fat crème fraîche as an alternative to double cream in this recipe.

SERVES 4 **PER SERVING 702** CALS **30.2g** FAT

Chicken, Pineapple & Mango Kebabs

PREP TIME 15 MINS **COOK TIME** 15 MINS

Light Lunch

- **4 chicken breasts, skinless**
- **1cm (½in) ginger, peeled and finely chopped**
- **small bunch of fresh mint, finely chopped plus extra to garnish**
- **juice and zest of 2 limes, plus 2 limes, quartered**
- **220g packet coriander-and-lemon couscous**
- **216g canned pineapple chunks in juice, drained**
- **1 mango, peeled and cubed**
- **sweet-and-sour dipping sauce, to serve**

1 Cut the chicken into bite-sized pieces and toss with the ginger, mint and the juice and zest of 2 limes in a non-metallic bowl.

2 Prepare the couscous according to the packet instructions.

3 Thread the chicken pieces, pineapple chunks, mango and lime wedges on 8 presoaked bamboo skewers. Place in a preheated griddle pan or grill and cook for 12–15 minutes, turning halfway, until the chicken is cooked through.

4 Serve with the couscous and sweet-and-sour sauce. Garnish with mint.

TRY THIS...
with a large green
salad on the side.

SERVES 4 PER SERVING 405 CALS 41.1g FAT

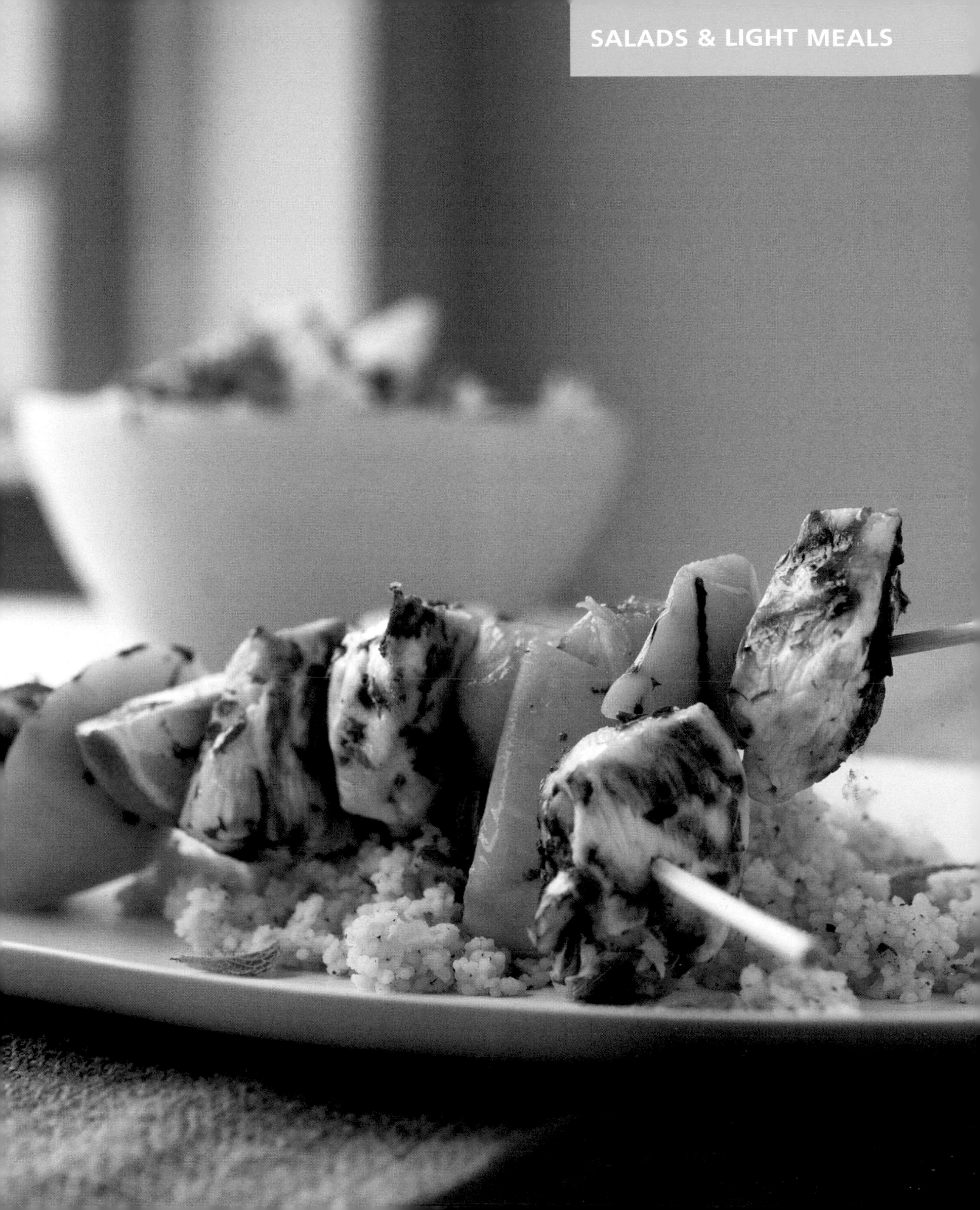

Asian Chicken Salad

PREP TIME 10-15 MINS **COOK TIME** NONE

Light Lunch

- 2 cooked, skinless chicken fillets, shredded
- 200g (7oz) beansprouts, rinsed
- 1 large carrot, shredded or grated
- 125g (4oz) Chinese leaves, shredded
- 50g (2oz) mangetout, sliced
- 3 tablespoons soy sauce
- 3 tablespoons smooth peanut butter
- 3 tablespoons honey
- 1 tablespoon cider vinegar
- ½ teaspoon ground ginger

1 Mix the beansprouts together with the carrot, Chinese leaves, mangetout and chicken.

2 Whisk the remaining ingredients together until smooth and drizzle over the salad before serving.

**!
CONTAINS
NUTS**

SERVES 4 PER SERVING 255 CALS 10.4g FAT

Warm Chicken Caesar Salad

Tasty Supper

PREP TIME 10 MINS **COOK TIME** 15 MINS

- 4 chicken breasts, skinless and boneless
- 2 tablespoons olive oil
- grated zest and juice of 1 lemon
- salt and freshly ground black pepper
- 1 head of cos lettuce, separated
- 2 tablespoons fresh parsley, chopped
- 25g (1oz) Parmesan cheese shavings
- ready-made croutons (optional)

FOR THE DRESSING

- 1 egg plus 1 egg yolk
- 1 teaspoon Dijon mustard
- salt and freshly ground black pepper
- 300ml (½ pint) sunflower oil
- juice of ½ lemon
- 2 anchovy fillets, drained and mashed

CHEF'S TIP

Sprinkle ready-made croutons with chilli flakes and heat through in a frying pan for an extra spicy finish.

1 Preheat grill to high. Whisk the olive oil with the lemon rind and juice. Season, then pour over the chicken, in a roasting tin. Grill, turning occasionally and set aside.

2 Make the dressing by putting the egg and egg yolk in a food processor with the mustard and seasoning. Whizz, then mix in the sunflower oil, lemon juice and anchovies.

3 Slice the chicken, toss with the lettuce, dressing, parsley and Parmesan and croutons, if using. Serve immediately.

SERVES 4 PER SERVING 704 CALS 59g FAT

Chicken & Mixed Vegetable Frittata

Family Tea-time

PREP TIME 5 MINS **COOK TIME** 15 MINS

- 350g (12oz) cooked chicken, skinless, cut into cubes
- spray oil
- 1 onion, peeled and sliced
- 1 garlic clove, peeled and crushed
- 175g (6oz) frozen mixed vegetables
- 4 eggs
- small bunch parsley, chopped, plus extra to garnish
- 1 teaspoon paprika
- sea salt
- cucumber and tomato salad, to serve

1 Heat a little oil in a non-stick 20cm (8in) frying pan. Add the onion and garlic and cook for 1–2 minutes, stirring continuously. Stir in the chicken and vegetables and cook for a further 3–4 minutes.

2 Whisk the eggs with the parsley, paprika and salt. Pour the mixture into the pan with the chicken and vegetables and cook for 6–8 minutes, or until the underneath is almost set.

3 Place under a preheated grill for 1–2 minutes or until the top is set. Serve in wedges with the salad.

CHEF'S TIP
Ideal for a family picnic as well as a nutritious addition to your child's lunchbox.

LOW IN FAT

SERVES 4 PER SERVING 266 CALS 9.1g FAT

Chicken Salad Niçoise

Tasty Lunch

PREP TIME 10 MINS **COOK TIME** 15 MINS

- 4 chicken breasts, skinless, cut into cubes
- 200ml (7fl oz) low-fat natural yoghurt
- 1 clove garlic, peeled and finely chopped
- bunch of herbs (eg, parsley, mint and chives), finely chopped
- 200g (7oz) green beans, trimmed
- 3 eggs
- spray olive oil
- salt and freshly ground black pepper
- 2 little gem lettuces
- 12 cherry tomatoes, halved
- ½ cucumber, sliced
- 1 red onion, peeled and finely sliced
- 75g (3oz) olives, pitted

1 Combine the low-fat yoghurt, chopped garlic and herbs together in a bowl. Chill until ready to serve.

2 Boil the beans for 3–5 minutes. Drain and refresh in cold water. Hard boil the eggs for 8 minutes. Leave to cool, shell and quarter.

3 Meanwhile, spray the chicken with a little oil and season. Place on a preheated griddle pan or grill for 10–12 minutes, turning halfway, until cooked through.

4 Place the lettuce leaves in a large bowl with the beans, tomatoes, cucumber, onion, eggs, chicken and olives. Add the dressing.

SERVES 4 PER SERVING 333 CALS 11.1g FAT

Rice Noodle Salad

PREP TIME 5 MINS **COOK TIME** NONE

Light Bite

- 150g pack cooked lime-and-coriander chicken
- 125g (4oz) rice noodles
- grated zest and juice of ½ lime
- 1 tablespoon soy sauce
- 1 tablespoon soft light brown sugar
- ½ red chilli, diced
- 1 large carrot, grated
- 25g (1oz) peanuts, chopped

1 Cover the rice noodles with boiling water and leave to stand for 4 minutes, then drain and rinse in cold water. Mix the lime zest and juice together with the soy, sugar, chilli and coriander, then toss this together with the noodles and grated carrot.

2 Divide between 2 plates and top with the chicken and peanuts. Serve immediately.

! CONTAINS NUTS

LOW IN FAT

SERVES 4 PER SERVING 436 CALS 8g FAT

Easy Chicken in Mustard Sauce

Quick Supper

PREP TIME 5 MINS **COOK TIME** 20 MINS

- **4 x 125g (4oz) chicken breasts, cut into strips**
- **spray oil**
- **6 large shallots, peeled and sliced**
- **1 tablespoon wholegrain mustard**
- **6 tablespoons half-fat crème fraîche**

1 Spray a large pan with oil and gently fry the shallots until they are transparent. Add the chicken and stir-fry for 6–8 minutes until the chicken is cooked and browned all over.

2 Remove from the heat and add the mustard and crème fraîche. Reheat slowly for about 3 minutes or until piping hot.

LOW
IN
FAT

TRY THIS...
With basmati rice or vegetable couscous

SERVES 4 PER SERVING 163 CALS 5g FAT

Warm Mexican Chicken Salad

Tasty Supper

PREP TIME 10 MINS **COOK TIME** 10 MINS

- 500g (18oz) chicken breasts, skinless
- ½ teaspoon hot chilli powder
- 1 tablespoon paprika
- 1 teaspoon dried onion powder
- salt and freshly ground black pepper
- 2 tablespoons vegetable oil
- 1 red onion, peeled and finely chopped
- 326g canned sweetcorn, drained
- a few sprigs fresh coriander
- 125g (4oz) prepared assorted baby salad leaves
- 2 avocados, stoned, peeled and chopped, in the juice of 1 lime
- 125g (4oz) tortilla chips
- 150ml (¼ pint) soured cream

1 Cut the chicken into strips and toss in a bowl with the chilli powder, paprika, onion powder and seasoning.

2 Heat the oil in a large frying pan or wok and stir-fry the chicken for 7–8 minutes until it is golden. Drain well and keep warm.

3 In another bowl, mix the onion, sweetcorn and coriander. Finally add the salad leaves. Toss the avocados and warm chicken into the salad, along with the tortilla chips. Serve immediately with soured cream.

SERVES 4 PER SERVING 604 CALS 32.4g FAT

Artichoke & Chicken Salad

PREP TIME 30 MINS **COOK TIME** 10 MINS

Family Lunch

- 200g (7oz) chicken breasts, skinless
- salad leaves, mixed
- 1½ tablespoons sunflower oil
- 1 red pepper, deseeded and sliced
- 280g jar artichokes, drained and cut in half lengthways
- 75g (3oz) sun-dried tomatoes, cut into strips
- 1 avocado, stoned, peeled and sliced
- 75g (3oz) marinated anchovy fillets

FOR THE DRESSING

- 2 tablespoons olive oil
- 1 tablespoon red wine vinegar
- ½–1 teaspoon Dijon mustard
- 2 tablespoons fresh parsley, chopped
- 2 tablespoons fresh basil, finely shredded

1 Cut the chicken breast into thin strips and place the salad leaves in the serving bowl.

2 Heat the sunflower oil in a large frying pan, add the chicken, red pepper, artichokes and sun-dried tomatoes and stir-fry for 3–4 minutes, until the chicken is cooked. Transfer onto the salad leaves, and add the avocado and anchovy fillets.

3 Put all the dressing ingredients into a small bowl and whisk together. Warm the salad dressing in the frying pan for 1–2 minutes. Pour over the salad and serve immediately.

SERVES 2 PER SERVING **597** CALS **36g** FAT

Chicken Quesadillas

Tasty Supper

PREP TIME 10 MINS **COOK TIME** 15 MINS

- 200g (7oz) chicken breasts, cooked and thinly sliced
- 8 flour tortillas
- 300g jar spicy salsa
- 1 bunch spring onions, chopped
- 150g (5oz) Cheddar cheese, grated

1 Lay out 4 of the tortillas on the chopping board. Spread each one with 3 tablespoons of salsa. Divide the chicken, spring onions and cheese between them, and top each one with another tortilla.

2 Heat a large non-stick frying pan over a medium flame. Add one tortilla sandwich to the pan and cook for 1½–2 minutes, pressing down firmly with a cooking slice, until the quesadilla is crisp and light golden brown on the bottom.

3 Remove pan from heat and place a large plate over the pan. Using oven gloves, turn the pan upside down to turn the quesadilla out on to the plate. Slide back into the pan, uncooked side down, and cook for a further 1½–2 minutes.

4 Repeat with the remaining quesadillas until all are cooked. Cut into wedges and serve with the remaining salsa.

CHEF'S TIP

Serve with a simple salad on the side using whatever salad ingredients you have to hand in an oil-and-vinegar dressing.

SERVES 4 PER SERVING 529 CALS 27.5g FAT

Herby Chicken Couscous

PREP TIME 10 MINS COOK TIME 12 MINS

Family Tea-time

- 4 x 125g (4oz) chicken breasts, skinless
- 250g (9oz) couscous
- 300ml (½ pint) hot chicken or vegetable stock
- 25g (1oz) butter
- 5 tablespoons olive oil
- 15g (½oz) frest mint, chopped
- 15g (½oz) flat-leafed parsley, chopped
- 2 sticks celery, chopped
- 3 garlic cloves, peeled and thinly sliced
- 75g (3oz) sultanas
- 50g (2oz) pine nuts, toasted
- salt and freshly ground black pepper
- 2 tablespoons lemon juice

1 Slice each chicken breast lengthways with diagonal cuts to make thin slices and season. Put the couscous in a large bowl, add the hot stock and leave for 5 minutes.

2 Add the butter and 1 tablespoon of the oil to the frying pan and heat until the butter has melted. Add the chicken and cook for 3–4 minutes on each side until cooked through.

3 Meanwhile, toss the mint, parsley, celery, garlic, sultanas and pine nuts with the couscous and season. Mix the remaining olive oil in a small bowl with the lemon juice. Spoon the couscous onto plates, pile the chicken slices on top and drizzle with the lemon dressing.

SERVES 4 PER SERVING 594 CALS 30.2g FAT

On the Hob

Chicken Liver Stroganoff

Lunch for One

PREP TIME 10 MINS **COOK TIME** 10 MINS

- 225g pack frozen chicken livers, defrosted
- 50ml (2fl oz) milk
- 1 tablespoon olive oil
- 1 small red onion, peeled and sliced
- 15g (½oz) butter
- 2 tablespoons half-fat crème fraîche
- 1 heaped teaspoon grain mustard
- 1 tablespoon fresh parsley, chopped
- salt and freshly ground black pepper

1 Rinse the chicken livers, place in a bowl with the milk and leave to soak for 15 minutes. Drain and pat dry on kitchen paper.

2 Heat the oil in a frying pan, add onion and cook for 2 minutes until softened. Push onion to side of pan, add the butter and let it melt. Add chicken livers to pan and cook for 1 minute on each side over a high heat until browned. Stir onion and livers together.

3 Mix in the crème fraîche, mustard and parsley and heat until bubbling and livers are cooked. Season to taste.

SERVES 1 PER SERVING 518 CALS 38.1g FAT

Spanish-style Chicken with Sherry & Peppers

Quick Supper

PREP TIME 2 MINS **COOK TIME** 13 MINS

- 4 chicken breasts, skinless
- 2 tablespoons olive oil
- salt and freshly ground black pepper
- 3 cloves garlic, peeled and sliced
- 150ml (¼ pint) dry sherry
- 150ml (¼ pint) chicken stock
- 290g jar roasted red peppers, drained and sliced
- 15g (½oz) toasted flaked almonds

LOW IN FAT

1 Heat the oil in a non-stick frying pan, lightly season the chicken breasts and brown for 2 minutes each side over a high heat.

2 Add the garlic and cook for 1 min, then add the sherry, stock and red peppers. Bring to a fast simmer, cover and cook for a further 5 minutes until the sauce has reduced and is slightly syrupy.

3 Scatter the toasted almonds over the chicken.

TRY THIS... with mashed potato and broccoli.

! CONTAINS NUTS

SERVES 4 PER SERVING 243 CALS 11g FAT

Smoky Chicken Hotpot

PREP TIME 10 MINS **COOK TIME** 40 MINS

Family Tea-time

- 2 chicken breasts, skinless and chopped
- 4 rashers streaky bacon, rindless and each cut into 3 pieces
- 1 tablespoon olive oil
- 100g (3½oz) chorizo sausage, sliced into thick rings
- 1 onion, peeled and sliced
- 1 red pepper, deseeded and cut into strips
- 400g canned chopped tomatoes
- 300ml (½ pint) hot chicken stock
- 1 tablespoon soft dark brown sugar
- 410g canned chickpeas, rinsed and drained
- 4 tablespoons fresh parsley, chopped
- salt and freshly ground black pepper

1 Heat a flameproof casserole dish, add the bacon and dry-fry for a few minutes, then add the oil and, when hot, add the chicken and chorizo. Cook, stirring occasionally, until the chicken is sealed and the pimiento oil is drawn from the chorizo.

2 Add the onion and red pepper, put the lid on the pan and cook over a medium heat for 5 minutes.

3 Add the tomatoes, stock, sugar, chickpeas and half of the parsley. Cover and simmer for 10 minutes, then take the lid off and simmer for another 15–20 minutes to let the sauce thicken. Season to taste.

4 Serve immediately, sprinkled with the rest of the parsley.

CHEF'S TIP
Chorizo is a delicious Spanish seasoned and smoked pork sausage. Packs are widely available.

SERVES 4 PER SERVING 437 CALS 20g FAT SUITABLE FOR FREEZING

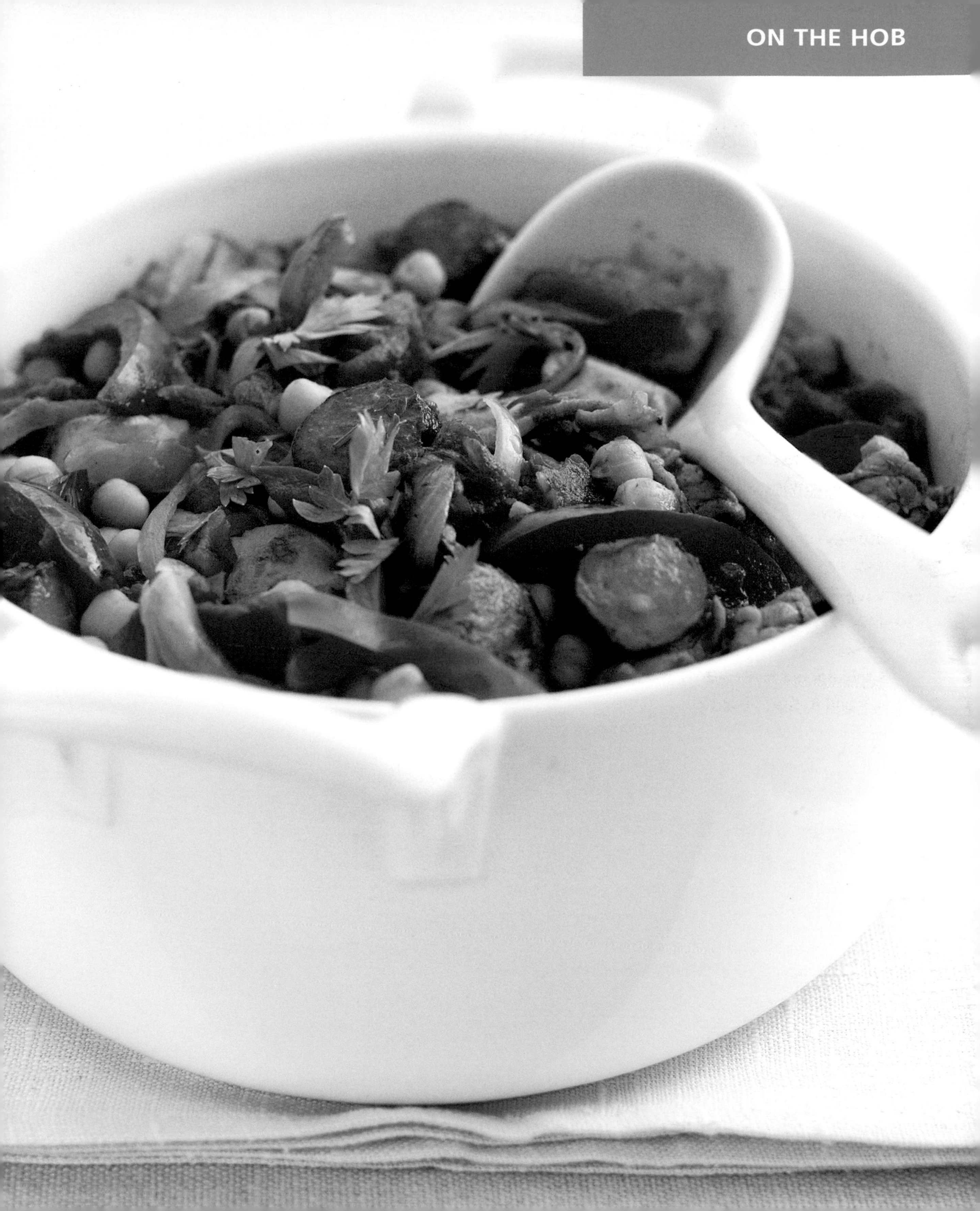

Italian Chicken with Olives & Peppers

Weekday Supper

PREP TIME 10 MINS **COOK TIME** 40 MINS

- **4 chicken legs**
- **1 tablespoon olive oil**
- **1 onion, peeled and sliced**
- **2 peppers, deseeded and sliced**
- **2 cloves garlic, peeled and sliced**
- **500g jar tomato and basil pasta sauce**
- **50g (2oz) black olives**

1 Brown the chicken legs in the oil for 5 minutes, then set aside.

2 Add the onion and peppers to the pan and stir-fry for 4 minutes, then add the garlic and cook for 1 minute more.

3 Stir in the pasta sauce and 200ml (7fl oz) boiling water. Return the chicken to the pan and stir in the olives. Cover and simmer for 30 minutes or until the chicken is cooked through.

TRY THIS...
with rice and green beans and garnish with parsley.

SERVES 4 PER SERVING 334 CALS 17.5g FAT SUITABLE FOR FREEZING

Belgian Chicken Stew

PREP TIME 15 MINS **COOK TIME** 20 MINS *Weekend Lunch*

- 4 chicken breasts, skinless
- 1 chicken stock cube
- 600g (1lb 6oz) small new potatoes
- 65g (2½oz) butter
- 2 large carrots, peeled and grated
- 2 large leeks, trimmed and shredded
- 40g (1½oz) plain flour
- 100ml (3½fl oz) double cream

1 Poach the chicken breasts for 15 minutes in a large covered pan, with 500ml (17fl oz) boiling water and the stock cube. Turn the chicken breasts over halfway through cooking. Meanwhile, boil the potatoes in a pan for 15–20 minutes or until tender, drain and keep warm.

2 Melt 25g (1oz) butter in a saucepan, add the carrots and leeks, plus 2 tablespoons water, cover and cook gently for 5 minutes.

3 Remove the chicken breasts to a plate, cover and keep warm. Decant the stock in a jug. Melt 40g (1½oz) butter in the same pan, then stir in the flour. Gradually add the stock, stirring until smooth, followed by the cream. Simmer for 3 minutes.

4 To serve, divide the vegetables between 4 deep plates or bowls, and place a chicken breast on top. Pour the sauce over the chicken and veg and garnish with chopped parsley.

SERVES 4 PER SERVING 610 CALS 28g FAT SUITABLE FOR FREEZING

Chicken with Cider Sauce

Weekday Supper

PREP TIME 15 MINS **COOK TIME** 25 MINS

- 4 chicken breasts, with skins on
- 2 tablespoons olive oil
- 1 small onion, peeled and chopped
- 125g (4oz) chestnut mushrooms,
- 120ml (4fl oz) cider
- 120ml (4fl oz) chicken stock
- 50g (2oz) frozen peas
- 3 tablespoons double cream
- 2 tablespoons fresh parsley, chopped

1 Heat oil in a large, heavy-based frying pan and fry the chicken, skin-side down for 5–6 minutes, until browned. Turn chicken over and add the onion and mushrooms to the pan. Cook for a further 3–4 minutes until the mushrooms are browned.

2 Add the cider to the pan and allow to bubble until reduced by about half. Add the chicken stock and simmer gently for 10 minutes.

3 Add the frozen peas to the pan with the chicken and cook for 2 minutes, then stir in cream and parsley and simmer for 1 minute more. Serve with boiled potatoes mashed with butter, milk and salt and pepper.

SERVES 4 PER SERVING 471 CALS 27.2g FAT SUITABLE FOR FREEZING

Coq au Vin

PREP TIME 10 MINS **COOK TIME** 25 MINS *Dinner Party Idea*

- 8 chicken thighs, boneless and skinless
- 2 tablespoons plain flour
- Salt and freshly ground black pepper
- 4 streaky bacon rashes, chopped
- 50g (2oz) butter
- 8 shallots, peeled
- 300ml (½ pint) dry red wine
- 150ml (¼ pint) chicken stock
- 1 bouquet garni, fresh or dried
- 225g (8oz) button mushrooms, wiped
- 2 teaspoons Dijon mustard,
- 2 tablespoons fresh parsley, chopped

1 Sprinkle the flour on a plate and season. Slice the chicken thighs in half lengthways and toss in the flour, then toss in the bacon.

2 Melt the butter in a large frying pan and gently fry the flour-coated chicken and bacon with the shallots, turning occasionally, for about 10 minutes until browned all over. Add the wine and stock and mix until blended.

3 Add the bouquet garni. Bring to the boil and simmer, uncovered for 10 minutes. Add the mushrooms and mustard and cook for a further 5 minutes, stirring, until tender and cooked through. Discard the bouquet garni.

4 To serve, spoon on to warmed serving plates and sprinkle with chopped parsley.

SERVES 4 PER SERVING 414 CALS 20g FAT SUITABLE FOR FREEZING

Creamy Tarragon Chicken with Grapes

Quick Dinner

PREP TIME 5 MINS **COOK TIME** 10 MINS

- **4 small chicken breasts, skinless**
- **salt and freshly ground black pepper**
- **1 tablespoon olive oil**
- **100ml (3½fl oz) white wine**
- **142ml pot double cream**
- **125g (4oz) green grapes, halved**
- **2 tablespoons fresh or 2 teaspoons dried tarragon**
- **rice, to serve**

1 Season the chicken breasts lightly. Heat the oil in a frying pan and then brown off the chicken breasts for about 3½ minutes each side. Pour over the white wine and allow to simmer for 1 minute.

2 Add the cream and cook for a further 2 minutes, stirring in the grapes and tarragon for the last 30 seconds of cooking.

3 Serve with boiled rice and a green salad dressed with vinaigrette on the side. Add any grape halves leftover to the salad.

CHEF'S TIP
If you are using dried tarragon add to the frying pan when browning the chicken breasts.

SERVES 4 PER SERVING 341 CALS 21.5g FAT

Chicken, Lemon & Thyme Risotto

Family Tea-time

PREP TIME 10 MINS **COOK TIME** 15 MINS

- 2 chicken breasts, skinless and cut into small diced pieces
- 350g (12oz) easy-cook risotto rice
- 1 litre (1¾ pints) chicken stock
- 1 tablespoon butter
- 2 leeks, trimmed and sliced
- 1 tablespoon olive oil
- salt and freshly ground black pepper
- 1 tablespoon fresh thyme, chopped
- ½ lemon, grated zest and juice
- 25g (1oz) fresh Parmesan, grated

1 Put the rice and stock in a large saucepan and bring to the boil. Cook uncovered, stirring frequently, for about 15 minutes or until all the stock has been absorbed and the risotto has a thick, soupy consistency.

2 While the rice is cooking, melt the butter in a non-stick frying pan. Add the leeks and cook for 5 minutes until tender, then remove to a plate. Pour the olive oil into the frying pan, season the chicken with salt and pepper and fry over a medium-high heat for 5–6 minutes or until cooked through and golden brown.

3 When the rice is ready, stir in the thyme, lemon zest and juice. Mix in the leeks and chicken, followed by the Parmesan cheese. Check the seasoning, then serve the risotto immediately in warmed bowls.

SERVES 4 PER SERVING 510 CALS 10.8g FAT

Cheesy Chicken & Mushroom

Tasty Dinner

PREP TIME 5 MINS **COOK TIME** 25 MINS

TRY THIS...
with mashed potatoes and green beans.

- 4 chicken breasts, with skin on
- 110g (4oz) goat's cheese,
- 1 tablespoon olive oil
- 4 smoked streaky bacon rashers
- 25g (1oz) butter
- 250g (9oz) chestnut mushrooms, sliced
- 1 level tablespoon plain flour
- 250ml (8fl oz) white wine
- ½ chicken stock cube, crumbled
- salt and freshly ground black pepper

1 Divide the goat's cheese into 4 and push a portion under the skin of each chicken breast. Heat oil in a pan, add the chicken breasts, skin side down.

2 Cook for 4–5 minutes over a medium heat until the chicken skins are golden in colour. Turn over and cook for a further 3–4 minutes. Remove from pan. Add the bacon to the pan and cook for 2–3 minutes, and remove.

3 Add the butter to the pan and heat until foaming. Add the mushrooms and cook for 2–3 minutes until starting to soften, then stir in the flour. Stir in the wine and 100ml (3½fl oz) water, bringing to the boil with each addition of liquid. Stir in the stock cube.

4 Return the bacon and chicken, skin side up, to the pan and cook for a further 10–15 minutes, or until the chicken is cooked through.

SERVES 4 PER SERVING 406 CALS **22.4g** FAT

Tomato Chilli Chicken & Cannellini Beans

Quick Lunch

PREP TIME 2 MINS **COOK TIME** 15 MINS

- 375g pack mini chicken breast fillets
- 2 teaspoons olive oil
- 2 teaspoons garlic purée
- ¼ teaspoon dried chillies, crushed
- ½ teaspoon dried rosemary
- salt and black pepper
- 400g canned cherry tomatoes
- 410g canned cannellini beans

LOW IN FAT

1 Heat the oil in a frying pan. Mix the garlic purée, chillies, rosemary and seasoning in a bowl, then toss with the chicken to coat.

2 Fry the chicken over a high heat for 3–4 minutes, until browned. Add the tomatoes, cannellini beans and 100ml (3½fl oz) water. Cover and simmer for 10 minutes. Serve with rice.

TRY THIS... with steamed rice.

SERVES 4 PER SERVING 271 CALS 5.8g FAT

Tarragon Chicken

PREP TIME 5 MINS **COOK TIME** 25 MINS

Weekday Supper

- 4 chicken breasts, skinless and boneless
- salt and freshly ground black pepper
- 2 tablespoons olive oil
- 1½ tablespoons cornflour
- 150ml (¼ pint) dry white wine
- 150ml (¼ pint) chicken stock
- 6 tablespoons double cream
- 3 tablespoons fresh tarragon, chopped

1 Wash and pat dry the chicken breasts and season on both sides. Heat the oil in a frying pan and cook the chicken for about 8 minutes on each side until golden and cooked through.

2 Remove the chicken from the pan with a slotted spoon and keep warm while you make the sauce.

3 In the same frying pan, blend the cornflour with the pan juices and gradually blend in the wine. Pour in the chicken stock and bring to the boil, stirring, until thickened. Simmer for 1 minute then add the cream.

4 Remove from the heat, season with black pepper and stir in the tarragon. Add the chicken to the sauce and heat through, spooning the sauce over the chicken, for about 2 minutes.

SERVES 4 PER SERVING 324 CALS 19.3g FAT

Stir-fries

- Chicken & Mushroom Chow Mein

- Sweet & Sour Chicken

- Stir-fried Eggs with Chicken & Mangetout

- Chicken & Root Vegetable Stir-fry

- Chilli Chicken Stir-fry

- Moroccan Chicken

- Chicken & Mango Stir-fry

Chicken & Mushroom Chow Mein

Quick Lunch

PREP TIME 5 MINS **COOK TIME** 8 MINS

- 1 chicken breast, cut into thin strips
- 1 tablespoon oil
- ½ teaspoon garlic purée
- 75g (3oz) beansprouts, rinsed
- 3 mushrooms, sliced
- 50g (2oz) mangetout
- 4 spring onions, sliced
- 150g pack straight-to-wok noodles
- 2 tablespoons oyster sauce

1 Heat the oil in a wok until smoking hot. Add the chicken and stir-fry for 3 minutes.

2 Mix the garlic purée, beansprouts, mushrooms, mangetout and spring onions and cook for 2 minutes.

3 Add the straight-to-wok noodles, oyster sauce and 2 tablespoons water. Heat through, stirring well, for 2 minutes. Serve immediately.

SERVES 1 PER SERVING 609 CALS 18.2g FAT

Sweet & Sour Chicken

Tasty Supper

TRY THIS...
with cooked rice
and extra ketchup
on the side.

PREP TIME 10 MINS **COOK TIME** 15 MINS

- 4 chicken breasts, skinless
- 1 tablespoon olive oil
- 1 onion, peeled and sliced
- 3 mixed peppers, sliced
- 1 x 435g can pineapple chunks
  in natural juice
- 1 tablespoon cornflour
- 2 tablespoons tomato ketchup
- 1 tablespoon light soy cauce
- 1 tablespoon white wine vinegar
- salt and freshly ground black pepper

1 Heat the oil in a wok or a large frying pan. Cook the chicken breasts for 10 minutes, turning occasionally to ensure they're cooked through. Remove from the wok and set aside.

2 Stir-fry the onion and peppers over a high heat for 2–3 minutes. Strain the pineapple cubes (reserving the juices). Add to the pan and cook for a further 1–2 minutes.

3 Mix the cornflour with a little of the reserved juice to make a paste. Next stir in the remaining juice, ketchup, soy sauce, vinegar and 135ml (4½fl oz) water. Season, pour into the pan with the pineapple mixture. Bring to the boil, stirring until it thickens.

4 Stir in the chicken and simmer for 5 minutes. Divide between 4 serving plates.

LOW IN FAT

SERVES 4 PER SERVING 278 CALS 5.2g FAT

Stir-fried Eggs with Chicken & Mangetout

Quick Lunch

PREP TIME 10 MINS **COOK TIME** 8 MINS

- 3 chicken breasts, thinly sliced
- 200g (7oz) mangetout
- juice of ½ lemon
- 2 tablespoons sunflower oil
- 4 spring onions, sliced
- 2 tablespoons soy sauce
- 4 eggs
- salt and freshly ground black pepper
- sliced red chilli, to garnish

1 Top and tail the mangetout, slice in half and mix with the lemon juice.

2 Heat the oil in a large wok and add the chicken. Stir-fry on high for 4–5 minutes or until just cooked through. Add the mangetout, spring onions and soy sauce, and stir-fry for 1 more minute.

3 Lightly beat the eggs with 2 tablespoons water and season. Add to the wok and stir-fry until the eggs are firm but still moist. Serve immediately, garnished with sliced red chilli.

TRY THIS...
with boiled rice
and sliced red chilli
and soy sauce on
the side.

SERVES 4 PER SERVING 291 CALS 13.7g FAT

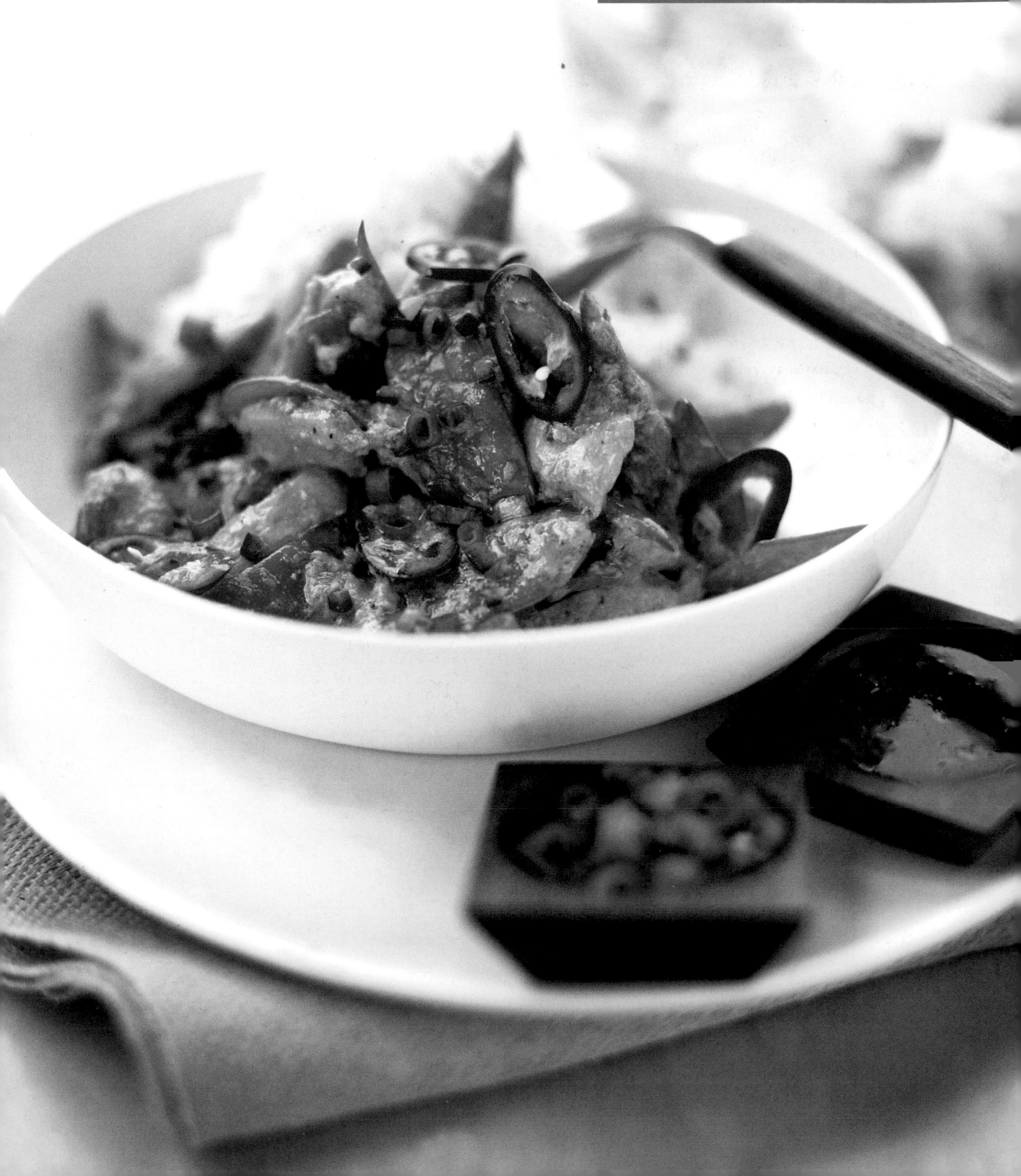

Chicken & Root Vegetable Stir-fry

Family Tea-time

PREP TIME 30 MINS **COOK TIME** 20 MINS

- 2 chicken breasts, cut into thin strips
- 1½ teaspoons cornflour
- 300ml (½ pint) chicken stock
- 3–4 teaspoons Worcester sauce
- 1½ tablespoons tomato purée
- 3 tablespoons vegetable oil
- 3 sticks celery, thinly sliced
- 2 onions, peeled, halved and sliced
- 225g (8oz) carrots, thinly sliced
- 400g (14oz) celeriac, peeled and coarsely grated

1 In a small bowl, blend the cornflour with the chicken stock, Worcestershire sauce and tomato purée.

2 Heat 2 tablespoons of the oil in a large wok or frying pan. Add the chicken strips and stir-fry over a high heat for 3–4 minutes. Remove from pan onto a plate and set aside.

3 Add the remaining oil to the wok, tip in all the vegetables and stir-fry over a high heat for about 5 minutes, until they are softened but still retain a crisp bite.

4 Return the chicken to the wok, including any juices remaining on the plate, add the cornflour mixture and bring to the boil, gently tossing the chicken and vegetables. Serve immediately with basmati rice.

SERVES 4 PER SERVING 366 CALS 13.7g FAT

Chilli Chicken Stir-fry

Tasty Supper

PREP TIME 8 MINS **COOK TIME** 11 MINS

- 2 x 250g (9oz) chicken breasts, skinless and cubed
- spray oil
- 1 red chilli, finely sliced
- 4 spring onions, finely sliced, plus extra to garnish
- 1 red pepper, deseeded and sliced
- 1 large carrot, peeled and sliced
- 75g (3oz) baby sweetcorn, halved
- 100g (3½oz) button mushrooms, sliced
- 4 tablespoons sweet chilli sauce
- 75g (3oz) beansprouts
- 300g straight-to-wok noodles
- soy sauce, to serve

1 Heat some spray oil in a large wok or frying pan. Add the chicken, chilli and spring onions and stir-fry for 2 minutes. Add the pepper, carrot, sweetcorn and mushrooms and stir-fry over a high heat for a further 5 minutes.

2 Add the chilli sauce, beansprouts, noodles and 2–3 tablespoons water. Simmer for 2 minutes. Toss the noodles into the mixture and heat through for a further 2 minutes.

3 Serve immediately with soy sauce and garnish with spring onions.

LOW
IN
FAT

SERVES 4 PER SERVING 335 CALS 6.9g FAT

Moroccan Chicken

PREP TIME 5 MINS **COOK TIME** 10 MINS

Easy Supper

- 4 chicken breasts, cut into strips
- 250g (9oz) couscous
- 300ml (½ pint) chicken or vegetable stock
- 1 teaspoon cinnamon
- salt and freshly ground black pepper
- 1 tablespoon olive oil
- 1 red chilli, sliced
- 25g (1oz) pine nuts
- juice and zest of 1 lemon
- herbed couscous, to serve

1 Put the couscous in a large bowl, add the hot stock and leave for 5 minutes. Toss chicken with cinnamon, salt and pepper, and stir-fry in hot oil for 6–8 minutes. Add the chilli and pine nuts and cook for a further minute.

2 Stir in lemon juice, zest and 6 tablespoons water. Let it bubble rapidly until slightly reduced. Spoon chicken and sauce over herbed couscous and serve immediately.

LOW IN FAT

SERVES 4 PER SERVING 214 CALS 9.1g FAT

Chicken & Mango Stir-fry

Quick Lunch

- 375g pack mini chicken fillets
- 2 tablespoons sunflower oil
- 1 red onion, peeled and sliced
- 1 red and 1 yellow pepper, deseeded and sliced
- 100g (3½oz) mangetout
- 1 teaspoon ginger purée
- 1 mango, peeled and cut into strips
- juice of 1 lime plus extra lime wedges, to garnish
- 3 tablespoons Thai sweet chilli sauce
- ½ tablespoon light soy sauce

1 Heat half the oil in a wok or large frying pan. Add the chicken and stir-fry for 5 minutes. Remove from the pan and set aside.

2 Add the remaining oil to the pan and stir-fry the onion and peppers for 2 minutes. Add the mangetout and ginger purée and cook for a further minute.

3 Return the chicken to the pan and add the mango, lime juice, chilli sauce and soy sauce. Stir-fry for 2 minutes. Serve immediately with noodles and garnish with lime wedges.

LOW IN FAT

SERVES 4 PER SERVING 265 CALS 8.4g FAT

Curries

Thai Chicken Curry

PREP TIME 5 MINS **COOK TIME** 20 MINS

- 480g pack cooked chicken breasts, skinned and cubed
- Spray vegetable oil
- 1 red onion, peeled and finely chopped
- 2–3 teaspoons Thai red curry paste
- 300ml (½ pint) reduced-fat coconut milk
- 100ml (3½fl oz) chicken stock
- 200g pack baby sweetcorn and mangetout
- saffron rice, to serve
- whole chillies and fresh coriander to use as a garnish

1 Heat some spray oil in a non-stick frying pan. Add the onion and cook for 1 minute. Stir in the curry paste and cook for a further minute.

2 Pour in the coconut milk and stock and bring to the boil. Add the chicken and veg, reduce the heat and simmer for 10–13 minutes.

3 Serve with saffron rice and garnish with a whole chilli and coriander leaves

SERVES 4 PER SERVING 262 CALS 11.8g FAT

Chicken, Potato & Coconut Curry

PREP TIME 5 MINS **COOK TIME** 20 MINS *Weekend Lunch*

- 480g pack ready-cooked roasted chicken breasts, skinned and cubed
- 1 tablespoon vegetable oil
- 1 bunch spring onions, sliced (plus extra, to garnish)
- 1 stalk lemongrass, finely chopped
- 1 red chilli (plus extra, to garnish)
- 400g canned reduced-fat coconut milk
- 3 tablespoons coriander paste
- 300g (11oz) cooked small potatoes, halved
- basmati rice, to serve
- fresh coriander, to garnish

1 Heat the oil in a non-stick frying pan. Add the spring onions and cook for 1–2 minutes. Add the lemongrass and chilli and cook for a further minute.

2 Pour in the coconut milk, stir in the coriander paste and bring to a simmer. Add the potatoes and chicken and cook for 10–15 minutes. Cook the rice according to the packet instructions

3 Scatter chicken with more chilli and spring onions and serve immediately with rice, garnished with coriander.

CHEF'S TIP
If any rice is left over, cover the dish with foil and store in the fridge for no more than a day.

SERVES 4 **PER SERVING 650** CALS **32g** FAT

Chicken, Chickpea & Red Pepper Curry

Tasty Lunch

PREP TIME 10 MINS **COOK TIME** 15 MINS

- 500g (18oz) chicken thigh fillets, bone-less and diced
- 1 tablespoon oil
- salt and freshly ground black pepper
- 1 red pepper, deseeded and roughly chopped
- 2 tablespoons curry paste
- 410g canned chickpeas, rinsed and drained
- 50g (2oz) creamed coconut, grated
- basmati rice and green beans, to serve

1 Heat the oil in a non-stick pan. Season the chicken and fry in the oil for 4–5 minutes, turning, until browned.

2 Add the red pepper and cook for 2 minutes. Stir in the curry paste and cook for 30 seconds, then add the chickpeas, coconut and 250ml (9fl oz) boiling water. Bring to a simmer, cover and cook gently for 5 minutes.

3 Serve with the rice and green beans and poppadoms on the side.

SERVES 4 PER SERVING 427 CALS 26.6g FAT

Quick Green Chicken Curry

Quick Supper

PREP TIME 10 MINS **COOK TIME** 10 MINS

- 4 cooked chicken breasts, skinless and cut into bite-size pieces
- 10 tablespoons fresh coriander, finely chopped
- 5 tablespoons fresh mint, finely chopped
- 2 garlic cloves, crushed
- 1 teaspoon ginger, finely grated
- 2 teaspoons ground cumin
- 1 teaspoon ground coriander
- 1 teaspoon caster sugar
- 1 green chilli, de-deeded and chopped
- 400ml (14fl oz) coconut milk
- salt and freshly ground black pepper

1 Place everything but the chicken and salt and pepper in a food processor and whizz for 2–3 minutes, until well blended.

2 Place the blended ingredients in a large non-stick frying pan or wok over a high heat. Bring to the boil, then reduce the heat and allow to simmer gently for 4–5 minutes.

3 Add the chicken to the pan and bring back to the boil. Reduce the heat and simmer gently for 3–4 minutes. Season with the salt and black pepper, then remove from the heat. Serve immediately with boiled white rice and lime wedges to squeeze over the curry.

SERVES 4 PER SERVING 295 CALS 18.5g FAT

BBQ & Griddling

Tarragon Chicken with Corn-on-the-Cob

Weekend Winner

PREP TIME	10 MINS + MARINATING
COOK TIME	1 HOUR

- 6 chicken breasts, skinless
- 2 tablespoons Dijon mustard
- 4 tablespoons fresh tarragon, chopped
- salt and freshly ground black pepper
- 6 tablespoons half-fat crème fraîche
- 6 corn-on-the-cob
- 1 tablespoon olive oil

1 Cut 3 slashes in each chicken breast. Mix the mustard, tarragon and seasoning into the crème fraîche. Toss the chicken breasts into the mixture to coat thoroughly. Leave to marinate for at least 2 hours, but preferably overnight.

2 Preheat the barbecue. Brush the corn-on-the cob with the olive oil and season lightly. Wrap each corn-on-the cob in foil and grill on the barbecue for 1 hour.

3 Add the chicken to the barbecue for the last 20 minutes, turning occasionally, until the juices run clear when the thickest part is pierced with a skewer. Serve the chicken with the corn-on-the-cob.

LOW IN FAT

SERVES 4 PER SERVING **287** CALS **7.7g** FAT

All-Weather Barbecue Chicken

Family Dinner

PREP TIME 10 MINS **COOK TIME** 55 MINS

- 4 large chicken legs, with skin on
- 75ml (3fl oz) tomato ketchup
- 15g (½oz) soft brown sugar
- 3 tablespoons clear honey
- juice of ½ lemon
- 2 cloves of garlic, peeled and crushed

1 Preheat the oven to 200°C/400°F/Gas 6. Slash through the skin of each chicken leg, then arrange in a large roasting tin. Roast for 30 minutes. Pour the excess fat out of the tin.

2 Whisk together the ketchup, sugar, honey, lemon juice and garlic. Brush the mixture over the chicken and cook for a further 25 minutes, basting a couple of times with the cooking juices, until beginning to caramelise.

3 Check that the chicken is cooked through – the juices should run clear when the thickest part of the leg is pierced with a skewer. Serve immediately with potato salad and mixed leaves.

SERVES 4 **PER SERVING 373** CALS **23.9g** FAT

Herby Chicken with Asparagus & Tomatoes

Light Lunch

PREP TIME 5 MINS **COOK TIME** 15 MINS

- 4 chicken breasts, skinless and boneless, halved horizontally
- 1 bunch fresh mixed herbs (eg, chives, parsley and basil), chopped
- juice and zest of 1 lemon
- salt and freshly ground black pepper
- 20 asparagus spears, trimmed
- 12 cherry tomatoes
- olive oil, to drizzle
- new potatoes, to serve

1 Toss the chicken with the mixed herbs, lemon juice and zest. Season to taste. Cover the mixture and set aside.

2 Preheat a griddle pan to hot and cook the asparagus and tomatoes for 5 minutes, turning occasionally (you may have to do this in batches). Set aside and keep warm.

3 Cook the chicken pieces on a hot griddle for 4–5 minutes, each side, or until cooked through. Slice the chicken diagonally and layer with the cooked vegetables. Drizzle with olive oil and serve with new potatoes. Garnish with chives.

LOW IN FAT

SERVES 4 PER SERVING 225 CALS 4.1g FAT

Griddled Chicken with Apricot Chutney

PREP TIME 10 MINS **COOK TIME** 10 MINS *Quick Lunch*

- 4 chicken breasts, skinless
- 250g (9oz) dried apricots, chopped
- 1 teaspoon sugar
- 1 teaspoon dried chilli flakes
- 1 tablespoon black mustard seeds
- 2 teaspoons white wine vinegar
- oil, for brushing
- potato wedges, to serve
- lemon wedges, to serve

1 Put the apricots in a pan with the sugar, chilli flakes, mustard seeds and white wine vinegar. Cook over a low heat for 10–12 minutes, or until soft. Set aside.

2 Heat a griddle pan until hot, brush with oil and cook the chicken over a medium heat for about 5 minutes on each side, or until cooked and the juices run clear.

3 Serve with the apricot chutney, potato wedges and lemon wedges.

TRY THIS...
with fresh rosemary sprinkled over the chicken and potato wedges.

SERVES 4 PER SERVING 213 CALS 2g FAT

LOW
IN
FAT

Barbecue Chicken

Tasty Lunch

PREP TIME 5 MINS + MARINATING
COOK TIME 20 MINS

- **4 chicken breasts, skinless and boneless**

FOR THE MARINADE
- **2 tablespoons brown sauce**
- **4 tablespoons tomato ketchup**
- **1 tablespoon Worcestershire sauce**
- **1 tablespoon olive oil**
- **1 tablespoon barbecue seasoning**

1 Blend all the marinade ingredients in a large bowl. Score the chicken flesh and place in the marinade. Stir well to coat evenly. Leave to marinate for 2 hours.

2 Place the chicken on a hot griddle pan and cook for 20 minutes, turning occasionally and basting with any remaining marinade.

LOW IN FAT

TRY THIS...
with a jacket potato and corn-on-the-cob.

SERVES 4 PER SERVING 211 CALS 5g FAT

Chicken with Lemon & Tarragon Pasta

Quick Supper

PREP TIME 5 MINS **COOK TIME** 15 MINS

FOR THE CHICKEN

- 2 chicken breasts, skinless and halved horizontally
- 1–2 tablespoons olive oil
- Salt and freshly ground black pepper
- 2 cloves garlic, peeled and finely chopped
- 2 vine tomatoes, cut into wedges

FOR THE PASTA

- 150g (5oz) tagliatelle,
- lemon juice to taste
- 1–2 tablespoons olive oil
- 15g pack fresh tarragon, chopped

1 For the chicken, heat the oil in a ridged griddle (or frying pan) until very hot. Season the chicken breasts, add to the griddle and cook for 10–15 minutes, turning. Add the garlic and tomatoes for the last minute or so.

2 Meanwhile cook the pasta according to the packet's instructions, then toss in the lemon juice, olive oil and tarragon.

3 Arrange the pasta in a neat pile on each plate. Cut the chicken into strips and lay over the top with the vine tomatoes. Season with salt and pepper and serve immediately.

SERVES 2 PER SERVING 595 CALS 14g FAT

Chicken Escalopes with Olive Butter

Tasty Dinner

PREP TIME 10 MINS + MARINATING
COOK TIME 30 MINS

- 2 chicken breasts, skinless
- 1 tablespoon olive oil
- 2 tablespoons fresh parsley, tarragon or oregano, chopped (or a mixture)
- ½ lemon, zest and 2 tablespoons juice
- freshly ground black pepper
- 25g (1oz) butter
- 4 green or black olives, stoned and finely chopped

1 Place chicken breasts between two sheets of clingfilm and beat out to about 5mm (¼in) thick with a rolling pin.

2 Mix the oil, half of the chopped herbs, the lemon zest and juice in a shallow bowl. Add some pepper. Coat the chicken in the marinade and leave for 30 minutes.

3 To make the olive butter, soften the butter in a small bowl and add the rest of the chopped herbs and the olives. Put in a small dish and set aside until ready to serve.

4 Heat a griddle pan to medium high. Press both escalopes on the griddle and leave for 4 minutes to ensure the chicken is sealed. Turn over and cook for another 3–4 minutes. Serve whole or cut into two or three pieces with the olive butter melting on top.

SERVES 4 PER SERVING 303 CALS 18g FAT

Texas-style Barbecue Chicken with Carrot

Weekend Lunch

PREP TIME 20 MINS + MARINATING
COOK TIME 20–25 MINS

- **4 chicken quarters, skinned**

FOR THE TEXAN DRY RUB
- **1 tablespoon sea salt**
- **1 tablespoon paprika**
- **1 tablespoon golden caster sugar**
- **1 tablespoon dry mustard powder**
- **finely grated zest of 1 lemon**
- **½ teaspoon cayenne pepper**
- **1 teaspoon freshly ground black pepper**
- **6 garlic cloves, peeled and crushed**

FOR THE SALAD
- **½ cucumber, cut into julienne strips**
- **1 carrot, coarsely grated**
- **¼ red cabbage, finely shredded**
- **3 tablespoons red wine vinegar**
- **salt and freshly ground black pepper**

1 Mix together the dry rub in a bowl. Rub over the chicken and leave for at least an hour, but preferably overnight in the fridge.

2 Combine the salad ingredients in a bowl. Season and toss together to mix well.

3 Cook the chicken on the barbecue or under a medium-hot grill for 10–12 minutes on each side, or until cooked through (when pierced with a skewer the juices should run clear). Serve with the salad.

SERVES 4 PER SERVING 223 CALS 4.8g FAT

Sandwiches & Wraps

Chicken & Spring Onion Burgers

Family Tea-time

PREP TIME 5 MINS **COOK TIME** 15 MINS

- 500g pack chicken mince
- 6 spring onions, peeled and chopped
- grated zest of 1 lemon
- 50g (2oz) fresh breadcrumbs
- 25g (1oz) freshly grated Parmesan
- salt and freshly ground black pepper
- 2 teaspoons oil
- 4 English muffins, split
- lettuce leaves
- potato wedges and relish, to serve

1 Mix together the chicken mince, spring onions, lemon zest, breadcrumbs, Parmesan and seasoning. Shape the mixture into 4 patties, each measuring about 10cm (4in) wide.

2 Pan-fry in oil over a low-to-medium heat for about 15 minutes or until cooked through, turning occasionally.

3 Meanwhile, lightly toast the muffins, then fill each with a burger and lettuce. Serve with potato wedges and relish on the side.

SERVES 4 PER SERVING 363 CALS 7.3g FAT

Chicken & Vegetable Wraps

PREP TIME 8 MINS **COOK TIME** 3-4 MINS

Lunch-time snack

- 2 cooked chicken fillets, sliced
- 1 tablespoon sunflower oil
- 350g pack stir-fry veg with peppers
- 2 teaspoons Cajun spice seasoning
- zest of ½ a lime
- 2 tablespoons fresh coriander, chopped
- 6 tablespoons soured cream
- 4 flour tortillas
- spicy potato wedges and salad, to serve

1 Heat the oil in a frying pan. Add the stir-fry vegetables and Cajun spice and cook for 3–4 minutes.

2 Mix the lime zest and coriander into the soured cream and spread over the tortillas. Divide the stir-fry veg and chicken between the tortillas. Roll up and serve immediately with potato wedges and salad.

SERVES 4 PER SERVING 290 CALS 11.8g FAT

Chicken & Apricot Burgers with Relish

Family Tea-time

PREP TIME 10 MINS **COOK TIME** 15 MINS

- 500g pack chicken mince
- 4 spring onions, trimmed and finely sliced
- 8 dried apricots, finely chopped
- salt and freshly ground black pepper
- 1 tablespoon olive oil
- pitta bread to serve

FOR THE RELISH

- 8 tablespoons Greek natural yoghurt
- 5cm (2in) cucumber, finely chopped
- 2 tablespoons mint, chopped

1 Mix the minced chicken with the spring onions, dried apricots and a generous amount of seasoning. Divide the mixture into four and shape each portion into a burger about 10cm (4in) wide.

2 Heat the oil in a frying pan and cook the burgers two at a time. Leave to cook over a medium heat for 5 minutes, pressing them down gently with a fish slice. Turn over and cook for another 5–6 minutes on the other side.

3 Meanwhile, make the relish by mixing all the ingredients. Serve the burgers with the relish and warmed pitta bread.

LOW IN FAT

SERVES 4 **PER SERVING 211** CALS **7g** FAT **SUITABLE FOR FREEZING**

Parmesan Crumb Chicken Breast Sandwich

Tasty Lunch

PREP TIME 5 MINS **COOK TIME** 10 MINS

- 2 chicken breasts, skinless
- 1 egg, beaten
- 50g (2oz) fresh white breadcrumbs
- 25g (1oz) freshly grated Parmesan
- 2 tablespoons olive oil

TO SERVE

- 2 ciabattas or other long crusty rolls
- 4 tablespoons mayonnaise
- lettuce, shredded
- tomatoes, sliced
- salt and freshly ground black pepper
- lemon wedges

1 Put the chicken breasts between 2 sheets of plastic film and beat them with a rolling pin to flatten slightly.

2 Tip the beaten egg into a shallow dish. In another shallow dish mix the breadcrumbs and Parmesan together. Dip each chicken breast into the egg, allowing the excess to drip off. Then dip the chicken in the breadcrumbs mix to coat, shaking off the excess.

3 Heat the oil in a large frying pan and add the chicken breasts. Cook over a gentle heat for 10–12 minutes, turning the chicken once, until cooked through and the coating is golden.

4 To serve, cut the ciabattas or rolls in half and split each horizontally. Fill each sandwich with mayonnaise, lettuce, tomatoes and a chicken breast. Season to taste and serve with lemon wedges.

SERVES 4 PER SERVING 346 CALS 2.1g FAT

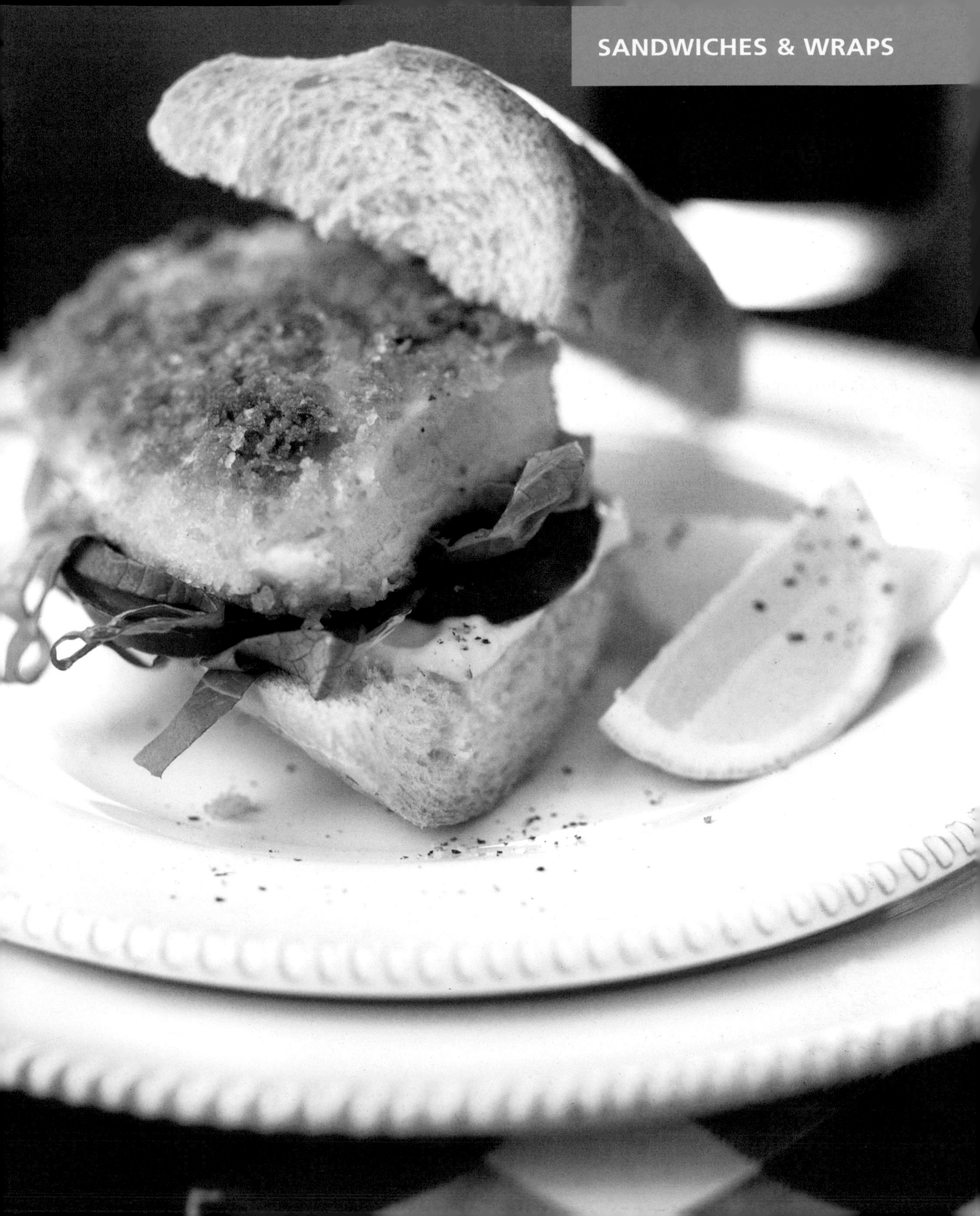

Chicken Tikka Mango Wraps

No-cook snack

PREP TIME 10 MINS **COOK TIME** NONE

- 200g pack cooked chicken tikka mini fillets, chopped
- 75g (3oz) soured cream
- 4 soft flour tortilla wraps
- 50g (2oz) iceberg lettuce
- ½ ripe mango, thinly sliced
- ½ red onion, peeled and thinly sliced
- Spicy potato wedges, to serve

1 Spread soured cream over each tortilla wrap. At one end of each tortilla, arrange the lettuce, mango, red onion and chicken in a line. Fold in the edges to contain the filling and roll the whole tortilla into a sausage shape.

2 Halve diagonally and secure with a cocktail stick. Serve with the spicy potato wedges.

SERVES 4 PER SERVING 238 CALS 7.7g FAT

Chicken & Avocado Salad Sandwich

PREP TIME 10 MINS **COOK TIME** NONE

Lunch on the move

- ■ **200g (7oz) cooked chicken breast, shredded**
- ■ **1 large ripe avocado**
- ■ **1 tablespoon lemon or lime juice**
- ■ **8 fresh mint leaves, shredded (optional)**
- ■ **8 slices mixed grain bread**
- ■ **12 cucumber slices**
- ■ **4 handfuls baby spinach leaves, rinsed and dried**
- ■ **salt and freshly ground black pepper to season**

1 Halve the avocado, remove the stone and scrape out the flesh onto a plate. Mash it with lime or lemon juice and add the shredded mint, if using. Spread the mashed avocado mixture over the 8 slices of bread.

2 Arrange the chicken evenly on 4 of the slices and season to taste. Put the cucumber slices on top and then the spinach leaves.

3 Place the other 4 slices of bread avocado-side down on top to make 4 sandwiches. Press slices together and cut each sandwich diagonally into two pieces.

SERVES 4 PER SERVING 397 CALS 16g FAT

Cajun Chicken & Blue Cheese Sandwich

Quick lunch

PREP TIME 3 MINS **COOK TIME** 8 MINS

- 1 chicken breast fillet
- juice of ½ lime
- 2 tablespoons Cajun spice mix
- 2 petit pain rolls
- 2 tablespoons light mayonnaise
- 2 ripe tomatoes, sliced
- 50g (2oz) Cambazola blue cheese, sliced
- Crisps, to serve
- watercress, to garnish

1 Cut the chicken in half horizontally to give 2 thinner pieces. Squeeze lime juice over and rub in spice mix. Place on a preheated griddle pan for 3–4 minutes each side, or until cooked through (when thickest part is piereced with a skewer, the juices run clear).

2 Split the rolls in half and spread with mayonnaise. Add tomato, cheese and cooked chicken. Serve with a handful of crisps and garnish with watercress.

SERVES 2 **PER SERVING 424** CALS **20.6g** FAT

Good practice for food safety and hygiene

- Always wash your hands before handling any food.

- Always wash fruit and vegetables before using them.

- Ensure your work surfaces and chopping boards are clean. Keep a separate chopping board for preparing raw meat.

- Read and follow the use-by dates on packaging and jars.

- Cool leftover food as quickly as possible, ideally within one to two hours and then store covered in the fridge.

- Leftover rice must be stored covered and for no longer than one day.

- If you are reheating food, make sure you heat all the way through and until it is piping hot. Do not reheat food more than once. Do not keep leftovers for longer than two days.

- Once thawed, do not refreeze raw food unless you have cooked it first.

- Do not buy cracked eggs.

- Children, pregnant women or the elderly should not eat recipes that contain raw eggs.

- Change and wash tea towels, towels, dishcloths, aprons and oven gloves often.

- Keep your pets off work surfaces and tables.

- Ensure that your fridge is 5°C or less and the deep freeze is at least -20°C.

- Organise your fridge so that meat is kept separately and on the bottom shelf. Keep dairy produce together and fruit, vegetables and salad ingredients in the salad compartment.

- Store raw foods separately from cooked foods to avoid contamination.

- After shopping, put all food for the refrigerator and freezer into their allotted places as soon as possible.